YOU ARE HERE

GRAPHICS THAT DIRECT, EXPLAIN & ENTERTAIN

From the Society for Environmental Graphic Design

Edited by Leslie Gallery-Dilworth, FAIA

Written by Gail Diebler Finke

ST PUBLICATIONS, INC.
CINCINNATI, OHIO

ISBN: 0-944094-32-5

To contact SEGD:
Society for Environmental Graphic Design
401 F Street NW, Suite 333
Washington, DC 20001
Tel. 202-638-5555
Fax 202-638-0891

Published by:
ST Publications, Inc.
Book Division
407 Gilbert Avenue
Cincinnati, Ohio 45202
Tel. 513-421-2050
Fax 513-421-6110

Distributed to the book and art trade in the U.S. and Canada by:
Watson-Guptill Publications
1515 Broadway
New York, NY 10036
Tel. 908-363-4511
Fax 908-363-0338

Distributed to the rest of the world by:
Hearst Books International
1350 Avenue of the Americas
New York, NY 10003
Tel. 212-261-6770
Fax 212-261-6795

Book design by Carole Winters
Art production by Rhinoworks, Cincinnati

Printed in China

10 9 8 7 6 5 4 3 2 1

CONTENTS

INTRODUCTION

Y ou are here! At the theater, the restaurant, the theme park, at the university, the museum, or the hospital. You are here in the airport, the train station or the metro. You are shopping, or visiting a resort. You are in the natural environment of a park, or on a busy street. But here is not so simple. Places were once easy to categorize by use and purpose. Now the distinctions are blurring.

Retail is entertainment. Entertainment may have an educational component. Educational institutions and entertainment facilities now often incorporate retail.

Exhibitions, no longer displays of static objects, may be interactive environments and resemble theatrical settings. Museums borrow more and more from shopping malls and theme parks. And there is the virtual environment. A physical place is no longer essential to shop, be entertained, visit a museum, or even engage in discussions within a public plaza.

The projects illustrated here have grown out of a variety of initiatives: transportation and urban planning, virtual information environments, tourism and economic development, civic celebrations, identity and branding, advertising and marketing, as well as education, entertainment, retailing, sales, sports and recreation. These projects originated in both the public and private sectors. All involve image, identity, branding, and communication. Many could be considered to qualify for more than one category.

The public sector and the private sector are learning from each other. Cities eager for the tourism dollar are rethinking how to promote and package their assets and attractions to become destinations. At the same time that public environments and authentic historic places are learning from the successes of the private sector, companies such as Disney are looking to history, and real events for entertainment and recreation. Authentic historic places have recognized the necessity of presenting themselves differently through repackaging, more engaging exhibits and activities, identity and branding, and making information more accessible.

Colleges, universities and healthcare facilities, all in highly competitive environments, have become more concerned about image. As they market to the public, first impressions of their facilities become more important. The ease with which people find their way influences their impressions.

Transportation, once the domain of traffic engineers and streets or public works departments, now joins with departments of tourism, planning, and economic development in considering street signs, gateways, and sequences of space as important elements in the presentation and life of the community. Train stations and airports are borrowing from shopping malls, food courts, entertainment centers, and museums.

When the Society for Environmental Graphic Design (SEGD) was formed 25 years ago, graphic designers, trained in the two dimensional environments of print, began working more and more in three dimensions. The designers of the projects illustrated in *You Are Here* come from converging and overlapping disciplines. They include graphic designers, architects, landscape architects, artists and sculptors, exhibit designers, interior designers, industrial designers, theatrical and set designers, art directors, and information architects.

You Are Here features award-winning projects. Each has been recognized for excellence by juries of the annual design competitions sponsored by SEGD. The images on these pages illustrate the design solution, but not the complex analytical processes involved in coming to these solutions. What you see in these projects is the tip of the iceberg. The graphics you see, the environment you experience, the organization and presentation of visual information, are the result of a critical analysis of diverse components, requirements and regulations. This process of reaching a visual solution to the problem, requires first identifying and defining the right problem. The creative, imaginative and analytical designers, whose work appears in this book, turn substance into image, and provide images with substance.

While Vitruvius is associated primarily with architecture, his criteria for good architecture can more aptly be applied to these projects, diverse as they are, as each embodies the principles of "firmness, commodity, and delight."

Leslie Gallery-Dilworth, FAIA
Executive Director
Society for Environmental Graphic Design

SECTION 1
WORK ENVIRONMENTS

Embarcadero Center

Places where people work require graphics that don't grow old when looked at by the same users every day, but that are readily found and understood by visitors. These two audiences can have very different needs. The designer's challenge is to address both while also communicating a consistent corporate identity and creating a system that can be easily changed, updated, cleaned and fixed.

Financial Guaranty Insurance Company

Sony Music Entertainment Headquarters

Lucent Technologies Global Sign Program

Interwoven bars decorating the signs for the renovated and enlarged Palmetto Exposition Center in Greenville, SC, represent the region's textile history, and add a stylish note to the otherwise plain rectangles. Bright colors add punch to the simple architecture, and make the signs visible in the cavernous space.

Design: Lorenc Design; Design Director: Jan Lorenc; Design Director: Chung Youl Yoo; Designer: Steve McCall

Client: Textile Hall Corp.

Architecture: HOK

Fabrication: Architectural Image Manufacturers

Photography: Rion Rizzo, Creative Sources Photography

Bright exterior signs complement the building's contemporary architecture, which features white stucco and simple shapes. The purple and yellow bands, symbolizing the area's textile history and the center's major clients, "bite" into the building.

Spotlights help the room signs to stand out.

Left: Red restroom and information nooks are color-coordinated signage disguised as interior decoration. The soffits, which hold lighting as well as signs, also lower the ceilings.

Below right: Integrated whenever possible into building soffits and bays, the signs must be bright and oversized to be seen in the building's vast empty spaces.

E dge-lit etched glass, porcelain enamel, full-matrix electronic displays, and other materials that many facility managers could only dream of are used lavishly at this 490,000-sq.-ft. convention center in Portland, OR. But the look is restrained and elegant, in keeping with the architecture and interior design.

Design: Mayer/Reed; Principal-in-Charge/Project Designer: Michael D. Reed; Project Designer: Tim Richard; Typographer: Debbie Fox Shaw

Client: Metro, Portland

Architecture: Zimmer Gunsul Frasca Partnership

Fabrication: CK Doty & Associates, Inc.

Photography: Strode Eckert Photographic

Interior signs made of edge-lit etched glass are mounted a variety of ways. Hung from the ceiling, mounted to the walls, or side-mounted to illuminated aluminum pillars, the signs do not sacrifice visibility to their restrained color palette.

The complex sign frames required expert manufacturing to manage the variety of materials and shapes, the electronics, and the many finished surfaces.

Exterior signs are made of porcelain enamel with elaborate metal frames. Their forms match the distinctive architectural style.

C urving interior walls provided the inspiration for these graphics, which give traditional New York City financial conservatism a stylish twist. Vinyl panels provide the flexible surface needed for this sinuous sign system, which can be changed at a moment's notice.

Design: Carbone Smolan Associates; Principal: Kenneth Carbone; Design Director: Claire Taylor; Designer: Kamol Prateepmanowong

Interior Architecture: Kohn Pederson Fox

Fabrication: ASI Sign Systems

Photography: Whitney Cox

A central column becomes an identity sign with the addition of a curving acrylic panel. The bronze letters match the curving brass handrail below.

Desk signs shaped like easels do the same job as their wall-mounted counterparts. The signs are not inexpensive, but they project an upscale image reassuring to visitors and employees alike.

Curving walls inspired the curving signs, achieved by pairing printed vinyl sheetings with a decorative metal assembly. The screw-and-notch mechanism holds the sheet in a space a little shorter than the piece, making it curve.

E nvironmental cues including lighting, color, and architectural forms replace traditional graphics in this 530,000-sq.-ft. convention center in Columbus, OH. Maps, video displays, and directional information are confined to five "monoliths" located at concourse intersections. The system explores new communication techniques in a style that matches its innovative architecture.

Design: Mayer/Reed; Principal in Charge: Michael D. Reed; Design Team: Debbie Fox Shaw, Michael Reed, Chris Ingalls

Client: Franklin County Convention Facilities Authority

Architecture: Joint venture between Eisenman Architects, Inc. and Richard Trott + Partners

Fabrication: Andco Industries, Inc.

Photography: ARTOG

Above: Taking cues from many influences, the building appears to be made up of many interconnected parts. The graphics inside reflect this organization, using visual cues such as color and light to communicate without words.

Opposite above: Like the architectural "forms" that seem to snake in and out of the buildings, signs labeling major areas seem to extrude from the walls.

Opposite below: Irregular "monoliths" at the five concourse intersections contain the bulk of directional information. Maps and video displays, as well as signs, convey information. Color and light signal shifts between meeting space areas.

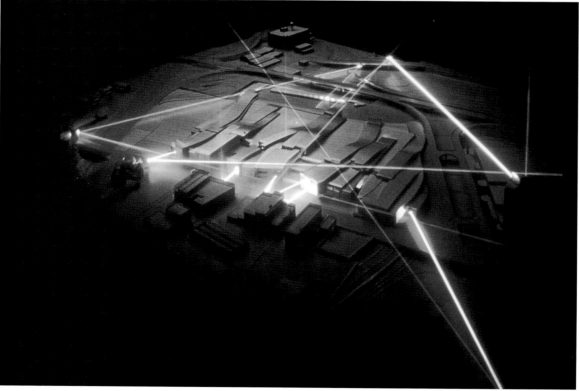

In Eindhoven, The Netherlands, this "Competence Centre" converted from an existing building introduces the public to the many technical innovations and products developed by Philips. Exhibits, computers, and films break the firm's work into eight technical "core competencies," and show how they work together to create diverse products.

Above: A variety of exhibition techniques, including interactive computer displays, introduce the company's complex technical work to the public.

Right: Documents, graphics, and artifacts create dynamic displays. The exhibits work with the high-tech look of the interior architecture to create a complete environment that communicates mastery of many technical and industrial subjects.

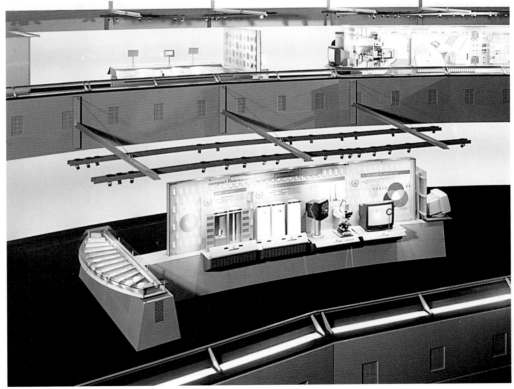

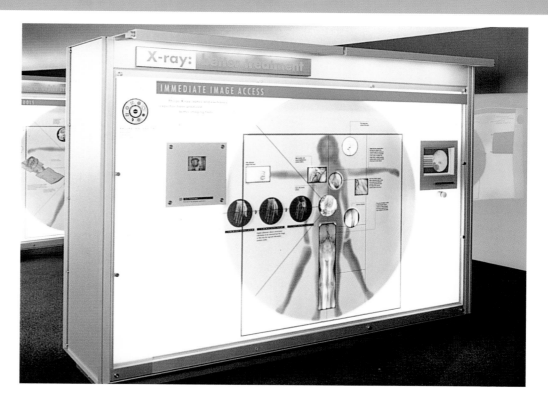

Bottom: Large displays like this one, for the company's improved x-ray machines, show how and why Philips products work.

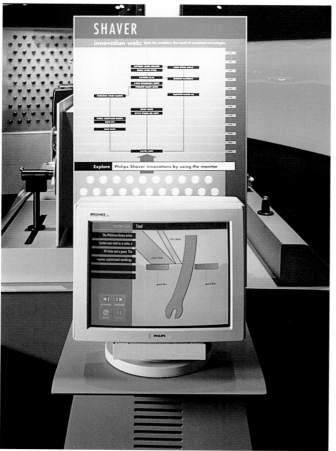

Design: The Burdick Group; Principals in Charge: Susan K. Burdick, Bruce Burdick; Associate/Project Director: Bruce Lightbody; Technical and Information Integration: Jon Betthauser; Designers: Johnson Chow, Jerome Goh, Cameron Imani, Jeff Walker, Steve Wiersema, Cindy Steinberg, Christopher Oppermann; Writers/Researchers: Aaron Caplan, William Smock

Client: Philips

Fabrication: Design & Production Incorporated, Gielissen BV; Carlton Benbow Contracts, Ltd.,

Photography: Herman de Winter

APPLE COMPUTER R&D CAMPUS

T he kind of fun and playful design that made Apple Computer famous marks the comprehensive interior and exterior graphics program for the company's Research and Development Campus. The project covers six buildings, with 850,000 sq. ft. of office space, on a 32.5 acre site in Cupertino, CA. It includes more than 3,000 room identification signs, code-required signs, building identification, and a major public art installation. Familiar Mac icons, typefaces, and bit-mapped graphics are all included in the brightly colored system.

Design: Sussman/Prejza & Co., Inc.; Principal in Charge: Deborah Sussman; Associate in Charge: Scott Cuyler; Senior Designer: Holly Hampton; Designer: Ron Romero

Client: Cupertino Gateway Partners/ACI Real Properties, Inc.

Fabrication: ASI Sign Systems, Carlson + Co., Superior Signs

Photography: Mark Darley, Annette del Zoppo

Top: Giant Macintosh icons sport in the sculpture garden, a public art installation that brings the familiar pictograms to life.

Middle: Each building sign used a number from a different Macintosh type font, in this case, a bit-mapped number 4. Each building's signs include the number and an identifying color.

Bottom: Interior signs include color-coded bands and the distinctive Mac fonts and icons.

MORGAN STANLEY WORLD HEADQUARTERS

The "supersigns" on Morgan Stanley's new American headquarters in the heart of New York's Times Square bring new life to an old building and a new image to the world's largest securities and financial management firm.

Design: Poulin + Morris, Designers: L. Richard Poulin, Douglas Morris

Client: Morgan Stanley

Architecture: Gwathmey Siegel & Associates Architects

Fabrication: Artkraft Strauss

Photography: Deborah Kushma

Morgan Stanley inherited strict requirements for large-scale, illuminated kinetic signs under the Times Square Redevelopment Area zoning regulations. Its solution was several giant signs.

While a financial company may not seem like a candidate for sign spectaculars, Morgan Stanley stepped up to the plate in fine Times Square style. The building's address alone is hard to miss.

At night, the building's facade is alight with bright signs. A map of the world tells the time in more than a dozen countries where the investment firm does business.

SONY MUSIC ENTERTAINMENT HEADQUARTERS

The design objective for this project, a new company headquarters building in New York City, was to create a cohesive visual impression while still expressing each company division's uniqueness. The designers created a distinctive modular sign system, then gave each division a bold color carried through the interior design.

Design: Poulin + Morris; Design Director: L. Richard Poulin; Designer: J. Graham Hanson

Client: Sony Music Entertainment

Architecture: Gwathmey Siegel & Associates

Fabrication: Signs & Decal Corp.

Photography: Deborah Kushma, Durston Saylor

The modular sign system, its look based on a CD "jewel box," is easily changed and can incorporate engraved and raised letters, as well as Braille messages. Its distinctive shape and colors give it a custom look.

Walls and photo murals of division stars are color-coded to celebrate their company division (Columbia, Epic, etc.).

Below: Sandblasted glass sign bands above the elevator and code-required elevator panels share the color coding. Bands of photographs of division stars are printed in tints of the division's color.

A spin-off of AT&T, multibillion-dollar Lucent Technologies is made up of 1,100 sites around the world. Its new identity emphasizes the name, which means "glowing with light." Its graphics are designed to be flexible, and to be easily fabricated, shipped, assembled, and replaced anywhere in the world.

Design: Landor Associates; Executive Creative Director: Courtney Reeser; Creative Director: Scott Drummond; Design Director: David Zapata; Senior Designer: David Oldman; Designer: David Rockwell

Client: Lucent Technologies

Fabrication (domestic): Architectural Graphics Inc. (AGI); Federal Sign; Philadelphia Sign Company; Signal Sign Company; Tandy Electronics, Sign Division; Thomas Swan Sign Company

Fabrication (international): Armada Janse BV; Colite International, Ltd.

Suppliers and Consultants: Horton Lees Lighting Design; Moss Machine; O&W Glass; Sign Management Consultants

Photography: Steve Calarco, David Oldman, David Rockwell

The Lucent identity standards feature modular signs made of luminous glass panels held on an articulated grid frame by cast aluminum armatures. They are designed to be replaceable, and can be made, shipped, and assembled anywhere in the world.

Above: Standards also include a related system for interior signs.

F lamboyant signs mark a flamboyant Melbourne building, beginning on the roof and extending throughout the center in giant-sized signs and supergraphics. Bright colors, jutting angles, and bold illustrations give this building great character, making it hard to tell where graphics end and architecture begins.

Design: Emery Vincent Design; Sign Designer: Garry Emery

Client: Melbourne Exhibition Centre Trust

Fabrication: Premier Graphics

Photography: Earl Carter

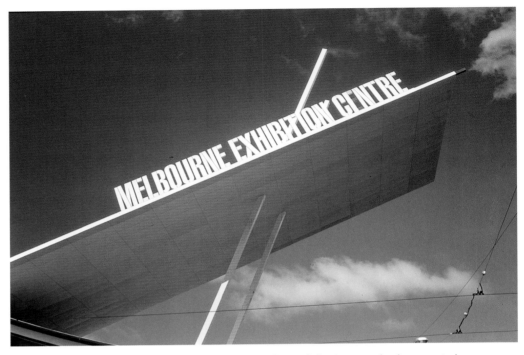

The building's sign seems ready to fly off the roof, held in place only by the two poles that spear its base.

Directional signs can be called restrained only in comparison with the rest of the signs.

Like giant blocks, the brightly colored signs jut through the walls and ceiling.

Originally a 1960s urban renewal project designed to combine commercial and residential spaces, San Francisco's Embarcadero Center needed an overhaul. The five-year project, begun in 1990, resulted in a comprehensive graphic system for the entire area, inside and out. It includes information kiosks, awnings and banners, signs, and lanterns, all of which were implemented throughout the six-block area.

Design: Poulin + Morris; Design Director: L. Richard Poulin; Designers: L. Richard Poulin, J. Graham Hanson

Client: Pacific Property Services, LP

Fabrication: Fireform Porcelain; Scott Architectural Graphics

Photography: John Sutton

Signs direct users to shops and restaurants.

Above: A comprehensive sign system connects all buildings in the area.

Left: Directional kiosks, inside and out, guide people to many different destinations.

GENSLER STUDIO 585

An alternate workspace for Gensler's San Francisco Retail and Graphic studios, this 2,800-sq.-ft., street-level space demonstrates the company's approach to design. There are workstations but no offices, and resources are shared. The conference room and entry facade feature giant typographic dingbats as window graphics.

Design: Gensler; Retail Design Director: Jeff Henry; Retail Project Designer: Michael Bodziner; Graphics Design Director/Principal in Charge: Jane Brady; Graphics Project Designer/Principal in Charge: Patti Glover

Fabrication: Martinelli Environmental Graphics

Lighting Consultant: Auerbach and Glasow

General Contractor: BCCI Constructions

Millwork: Design Workshops

Photography: David Wakely

Giant typographic dingbats ornament the entry facade windows. Only a small "sign" — knee-level window graphics in the lower right — identifies the studio.

Nontraditional graphics are scattered throughout the studio. There are individual workstations and shared work areas, but no offices.

FOOD BANK DONOR WALL

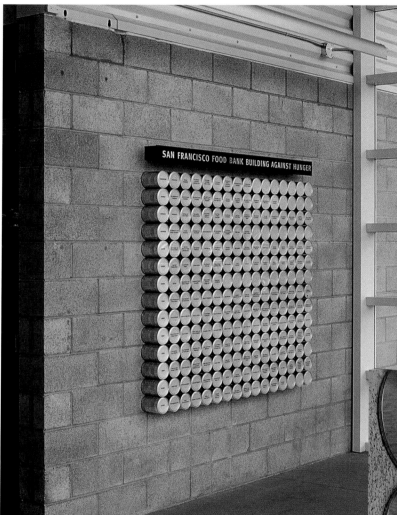

S ometimes the simplest materials make the biggest statements. This donor wall is made of tin cans. Located at the main entry to the San Francisco Food Bank, it reminds visitors that donors literally "build against hunger."

Design: Skidmore, Owings & Merrill LLP; Principal in Charge: Lonny Israel; Design Team: Lonny Israel, Jeremy Regenbogen

Fabricator: Thomas Swan Sign Co.

Made of tin cans, the donor wall for a food bank graphically represents the building's purpose and the importance of donation.

A simple grid identifies donors by name and the size of their gifts. Sandblasted blue acrylic circles, printed on the backs, identify donors. Clear acrylic circles are used to identify donor levels.

Glass and steel signs give an industrial character to this jeans manufacturer's corporate offices in Australia. Simple, but stylish, they capture the essence of the company's product.

Design: Emery Vincent Design; Principal in Charge: Garry Emery

Sandblasted glass panels at the Blue Café create an industrial look. They match the building's identity signs.

The cafe's sign, a screenprinted stainless steel sheet, combines simple industrial materials with stylish design.

Directional signs continue the spare, industrial look.

SECTION 2
HEALTHCARE AND INSTITUTIONAL ENVIRONMENTS

Science, Industry and Business Library

Though the word "institutional" has become a synonym for the uninspired and bureaucratic, design for institutions requires a demanding mix of pragmatism and creativity. Often daunting in size and complexity, these projects require designers with the vision and skill to make them comprehensible and enjoyable to visitors and employees alike.

Perry Community Educational Village

Pierpont Morgan Library

Royal Alexandra Children's Hospital

↑ EMERGENCY – Left Lane
↑ Main Entrance – Right Lane
↑ Visitor Parking
← Ambulance
→ Medical Offices

Bold sign colors and shapes were inspired by the building-block look of the hospital, which features a giant red wall and huge expanses of windows. The massive building sprawls over its Ocoee, FL, site, giving it a long, low profile that the signs also imitate.

Design: Tom Graboski Associates Inc.; Principal: Tom Graboski; Project Manager/Designer: Chris Rogers

Fabrication: Federal Sign

Photography: Tom Graboski

Above: Red and white signs mimic distinctive architectural features of the hospital, which has a high-tech but friendly look. Exterior signs are internally illuminated at night.

Opposite right: The exterior signs are studies in form and color from all angles.

Opposite below: Small signs cannot function on a building this massive and distinctive. A bold and interesting design is imperative.

DONOR RECOGNITION SYSTEM *at Art Center College of Design*

The lowly pencil, the fundamental tool of every art student, takes on prime importance in this innovative donor wall. Each donor to the famed Pasadena, CA, design school also receives a matching pencil and glass holder in a custom wood box.

Design: Dennis S. Juett & Associates Inc.; Designer: Dennis Scott Juett

Fabrication: Kandle Kings, R.S. Boles Fabrication, Sign Designers, Sign Pac

Photography: Magnus Stark; Roger Marshuts

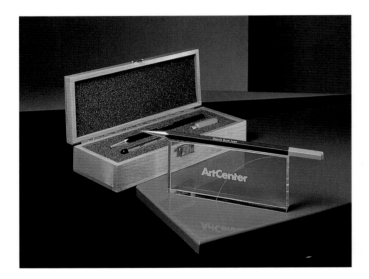

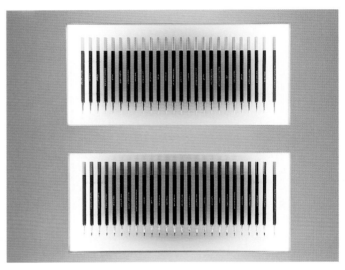

Above left: Donors receive matching pencils (stored in custom wood boxes) and glass displays.

Below: Major donors are recognized with anodized aluminum pencils etched with their names and displayed in built-in, illuminated cases.

PENROSE TILE INSTALLATION *at Carleton College*

The tile floor decorating the main lobby in the new Center for Math & Computing in Northfield, MN, is not only attractive, it also demonstrates a mathematical principle that every freshman class studies. The "Penrose" tile pattern was created by Roger Penrose, Rouse Ball Professor of Mathematics at the University of Oxford. Using Penrose's pattern ensures that the building literally becomes part of the curriculum.

Design: Cambridge Seven Associates; Principal in Charge: Peter Kuttner; Design Team: Ron Baker, Bobbie Oakley, Julie Dupre, Diane Norris, Denise Tran, Design Team

Associated Architects: SMSQSE

Fabrication: Twin City Tile and Marble; Creative Edge Corp.; Buchtal Tile

Consultant: Gene Walsh, Shep Brown, Inc.

Photography: Steven Bergerson

The building's contemporary style required a contemporary look for its lobby.

The floor tile illustrates a mathematical principle through non-repetitive, periodic tiling. The same simple shapes, colored differently, create an intriguing design combining mathematics and art.

H andcrafted brass signs in three custom-finished patinas complement the New York City library's architectural renovation. A special textured background adds to the elegant effect.

Design: Carbone Smolan Associates; Principal: Kenneth Carbone; Design Director: Beth Bangor

Architecture: Voorsanger Associates

Fabrication: Metalforms; Signs + Decal Corp.

Photography: Paul Warchol

Left: Understated elegance marks the exterior signs.

Opposite right: Shaped like a book stand, this sign at the entry discreetly asks for donations.

All interior signs, whether directional or interpretive, are made of brass. The textured background and three custom patinas match the classic architectural and interior design.

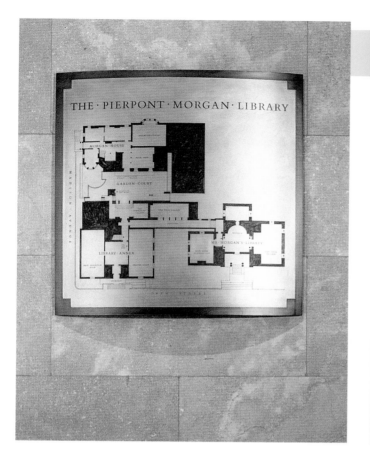

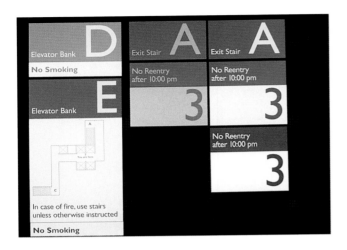

A mixed-use addition that brought the New York City complex to almost 1.9 million sq. ft. prompted a new wayfinding system. A single typeface in various thicknesses is the key to this complex, modular sign system that unifies four institutes. It provides a reassuring constant among the seemingly countless signs, which are made in many different sizes and of many materials.

Design: Poulin + Morris: Principals in Charge/Designers: L. Richard Poulin, Douglas Morris

Architecture: Polshek and Partners Architects

Fabrication: King Products, Inc.; Signs + Decal Corp.

Photography: Jeff Goldberg/ESTO; Deborah Kushma

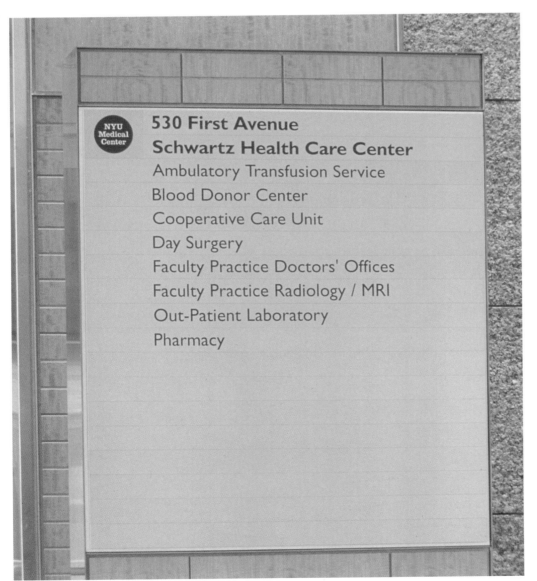

Above: Code-required "back of the house" signs continue the same look and typeface (Gill Sans), keeping the graphics consistent.

Left: Modular exterior signs appear to be permanent at first glance. The center's logo is visible but unobtrusive.

Opposite above: Spare lines and elegant materials fit well with numerous architectural styles.

Opposite below: Overhead signs direct patients and visitors to offices, departments, laboratories, schools, and even streets. The modular signs can be changed when departments and offices move.

Colorful signs and banners at the many library branches trumpet its centennial.

A celebratory graphics program and new visual identity helped usher in the Library's second century. Through playful letter forms, the graphics build on the library's past, emphasize its present, and project its future.

Design: Chermayeff & Geismar, Inc.; Design Director: Steff Geissbuhler; Designer: Emanuela Frigerio

Client: The New York Public Library

Production: New York Public Library Graphics Office; Hope Van Winkel

The New York Public Library   Celebrating Its Second Century

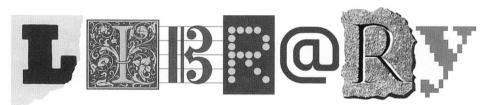

Left: The visual identity uses many different letters to explore its past, present and future.

Below: The identity lends itself equally well to merchandise and packaging.

Like a set from a 1920s film, the "Education Village" boasts sleek lines and dignified graphics.

For this new high school campus in Perry, OH, designers created a unified graphic system that matches the "futuristic" look of the architecture and the state-of-the-art educational techniques used within. By demonstrating commitment to young people, the center's spare and stylish design also tells students that the community expects much of them.

Design: Perkins & Will Environmental Graphic Design; Project Manager: James Woods; Designer: Anita R. Ambriz

Client: Perry Community Educational Village, Middle School and High School

Fabrication: Poblocki & Sons; Brilliant Electric Sign Co., Eder Banner Co.

Photography: Jim Steinkamp, Steinkamp/Ballogg Photography

Above: Integrated into the metal fence, cut metal letters decorate the stadium.

Left: The grown-up signs haven't forsaken juvenile sports. Banners and signs throughout the campus carry the team mascot, a pirate.

This $250,000 signage program designed to the Northampton, MA, campus's image is based on the area's many wrought iron fences, and the campus's original design as a botanical garden. It gives a friendly face to beautiful but unmarked terrain that students once had to navigate with maps in hand.

Design: Jon Roll & Associates; Project Manager/Designer: Sharon Stafford; Designer: Eric Beacom; Project Manager/Implementation: Debra Sherman

Client: Smith College Physical Plant

Fabrication: Design Communications, De Angelis Ironwork

Photography: Marvin Lewiton

Above left: A campus map is placed low and at an angle, so that viewers can look up and see the landmarks around them.

Above right: The restrained design fits the Ivy League school's image. Green sign faces and custom, wrought-iron poles recall the campus's original design as a botanical garden, and also fit it into a larger regional vernacular.

THE SCRIPTURE WALL *Saddleback Valley Community Church*

Biblical inscriptions cover the facade of a new church in Saddleback Valley, CA. On the 165 x 20-ft. glass wall, texts are grouped thematically and structured in a loose, poetic manner. People must pass through the wall to come inside, symbolizing the church's relationship to the scripture.

Design: BJ Krivanek Art + Design; *Design Director:* BJ Krivanek; *Designers:* Joel Breaux, Martha Najera

Client: Saddleback Valley Community Church; Pastor Rick Warren

Architecture: LPA, Inc.

Fabrication: Bro Designed Construction

Photography: Jeff Kurt Petersen

Biblical texts are loosely and pleasingly arranged on the church's glass facade. Etched into the surface, they evoke a quiet and contemplative mood.

The nontraditional arrangement of quotations invites viewers to take another look at words they think they know, and also intrigues the visitor unfamiliar with the Bible.

Quiet restraint and permanence were the design objectives for the signs for this 3,000-sq.-ft. university building in Tacoma, WA. Graphics identify major donors and sign a concert hall, rehearsal spaces, faculty studios, practice rooms and classrooms. Musical notation and motifs inspired the directional signs, and hand-chiseled letters in walls throughout the space integrate graphics with architecture.

Opposite above: In the building's light-filled lobby, glass donor signs with bass clef-shaped supports were inspired by the Chihuly rose art glass installation.

Opposite below: Signs shaped like sheets of music on music stands are used for floor directories and directional signs, while letters hand-chiseled into wood, plaster, and stone walls unify graphics and architecture.

Right: A variety of musical motifs decorate room identity signs, which also incorporate raised and Braille text to meet ADA standards.

Design: Mayer/Reed; Principal in Charge: Michael D. Reed; Design Team: Debbie Fox Shaw, Tom Shaw

Client: Pacific Lutheran University

Fabrication/Consultants: Doty + Associates; Trovo Design Works; Ostrom Co.

Photography: Strode Eckert Photographic

A 120-sq.-ft., programmable LED board at one end of the Commons area delivers sophisticated static and video messages, while bulletin boards offer low-tech areas for notices and posters.

The architects restored Memorial Hall, a Gothic architectural landmark, and transformed it into a student social center and dining hall. The second floor great hall offers formal dining, while the Commons below offers informal dining and space to hang out. Bulletin boards, an LED frieze, and a programmable LED board with video capability offer traditional and contemporary sign choices.

Design: Venturi, Scott Brown and Associates; Partner in Charge: Robert Venturi; Project Manager: Daniel McCoubrey; Project Architect: Richard Stokes

Client: Harvard University

Architecture: Bruner/Cott & Associates; Robert G. Neiley

Contractor: A.J. Martini, Inc.

LED Signs: Sunrise Systems, Inc.

Photography: Matt Wargo

Bulletin boards are prominent and well lit, making them useful to as many students as possible.

F ew things are as frightening for children and their parents as a hospital visit. These bright, three-dimensional signs for a Sydney, Australia, hospital help create a friendly atmosphere.

Design: Emery Vincent Design; Sign Designer: Garry Emery

Client: Royal Alexandra Children's Hospital

Fabrication: Central Signs

Photography: Earl Carter

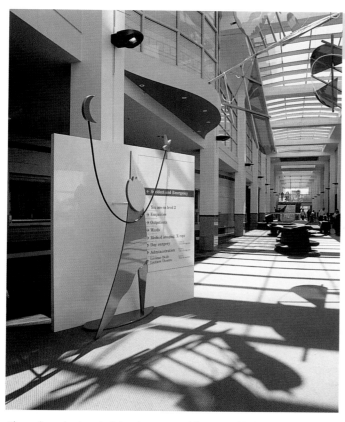

Throughout the hospital, bright oversized figures add cheer to the major directional signs.

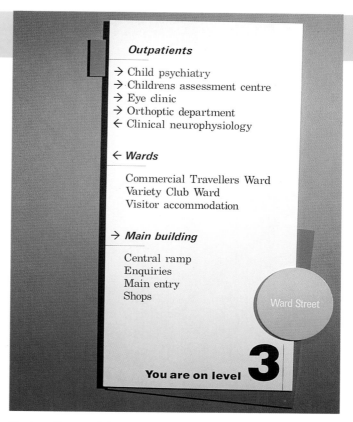

Outpatients
→ Child psychiatry
→ Childrens assessment centre
→ Eye clinic
→ Orthoptic department
← Clinical neurophysiology

← *Wards*

Commercial Travellers Ward
Variety Club Ward
Visitor accommodation

→ *Main building*

Central ramp
Enquiries
Main entry
Shops

Ward Street

You are on level 3

Simple wall-mounted directional signs maintain the playful design with colored circles and faux shadows.

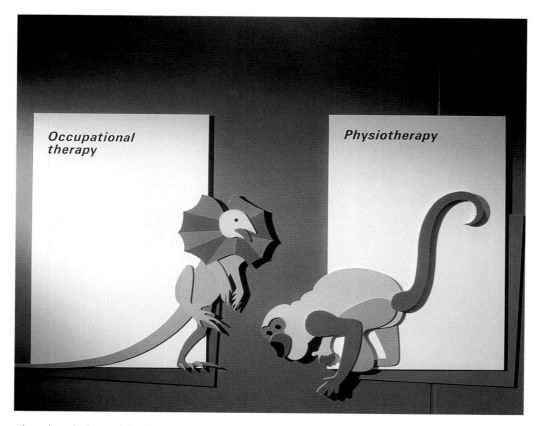

Occupational therapy

Physiotherapy

Throughout the hospital, bright oversized figures add cheer to the major directional signs.

L ocated in the venerable B. Altman Department store building, the New York Public Library's new branch is the world's largest computer library. Extensive graphics integrated with the innovative architecture by Gwathmey Siegel help bring the feel of traditional text to a facility that relies extensively on computers.

Design: Spagnola & Associates; Principal: Tony Spagnola; Associate/Project Designer: James Dustin; Project Designer: Robert Callahan

Client: New York Public Library

Building Architect: Gwathmey Siegel & Associates

Fabrication: Signs + Decal Corp.; Walter Sign Corp.; Sunrise Systems Inc.

Sandblasting: Carved Glass by Shefts

Photography: Christopher Little; Peter Aaron/Esto

Above: A curved soffit over the information desk contains LED signs and acts as the base for a "sign" made of dimensional metal letters.

Opposite above: Donors are identified on this curving sign wall, which subtly recalls computer screens.

Opposite below left: A curving wall of quotations 9 ft. high and 130 ft. long soars over patrons' heads, bringing the architecture to human scale and reinforcing the former department store building's new purpose.

Opposite below center: Metal text in the terrazzo floor identifies major library benefactors. Like many of the signs, it's integral to the architecture.

Opposite below right: Room and stack signs, in simple black and white, are modular for quick changes.

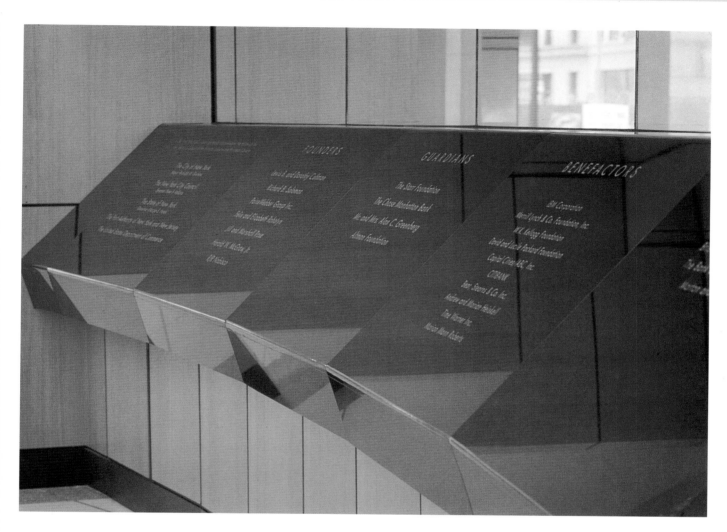

I nspired by the hospital's new logo, but not wanting to simply reproduce it, the designers came up with a coloring book theme. Giant crayons — some of them supports for the signs — decorate the signs, which depict brightly colored stick-figure children. Several signs include fiberoptic lighting.

Design: HKS Inc.; Director: Cris Coe; Designer: Nancy Goldburg

Fabrication: Architecture Graphics Inc. (AGI)

Photography: Roger Bell

The sign that set the theme for all the rest, this "coloring book" sign is designed to appeal to children, and to reassure them that the hospital is a good place. A Masonic emblem in the lower left corner is lit to give it greater prominence.

At night, the fiberoptic sign on the hospital's facade glows against the Dallas skyline.

Giant crayons are really supports for this sign, which depicts a happy child.

MASSACHUSETTS GENERAL HOSPITAL

A new wayfinding system for the complex of 18 public hospital buildings takes advantage of its recent redesign, which created a unified network of ground-floor corridors and lobbies. Instead of using building names, the new system is based on "routes" and "stops," like a subway system. People use ground-floor "routes" to find their "stop" — usually, an elevator that takes them to their final destination.

Design: Two Twelve Associates; Design Director: David Gibson; Senior Designer/Project Manager: Cynthia Poulton

Wayfinding Consultant: Sylvia Harris

Fabrication: ASI Sign Systems; Wallach Glass Studio; Kassindorf Carved Glass; Kraus & Sons; Livart, Inc.

Photography: Kevin Burke

Color-coded "routes" guide people through a new ground-floor system of corridors and lobbies connecting the 18 buildings in the hospital campus.

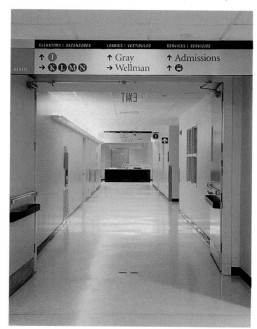

Most people use the system to find the elevator that takes them to their final destination. Like subway graphics, the wayfinding program gets people to the right "stop." From there, building graphics guide users to departments and offices.

LEISURE FACILITIES

Gund Arena

G ood design — in the sense of outstanding graphics and a definite, defining style — is almost a given at leisure facilities. Theme parks have set the standard for places people visit to "get away from it all." But in these projects, the practical side of environmental graphic design is forgotten at the designer's peril. Signs need to make visitors feel safe, secure, and in good hands at all times, whether they're looking for an attraction, an exit, or a rest room.

The Good Diner

The Trocadero

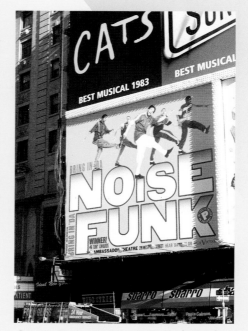

Bring in 'Da Noise, Bring in 'Da Funk Murals

THE SALAD BOWL

The neon sign for this casual restaurant sets the tone for the decor inside.

G iant bowls and fruits, reminiscent of French pottery, brighten this New York City restaurant's long dark eating area. The low-budget project relies on plasterboard and paint for its impact.

Design and Murals: Art Color Design, Susan Roberts

Architecture: Boyd Associates; Principal: Hugh A. Boyd

Sculptor: Alfred de la Houssaye

Fabrication: Hamilton Woodworking; Commercial Stainless; The Lighting Practice/Alfred Borden IV

Photography: Dub Rogers

Opposite above and below: A salad bar and the front desk are the long, narrow restaurant's only other features.

Giant bowls made of painted plasterboard recall French pottery and Matisse cutouts.

HOTEL HANKYU INTERNATIONAL

The design standards for this luxury hotel in Osaka include symbols, an alphabet, and decorative motifs. Designers created six stylized flower symbols, one for each floor, and a custom typeface.

Design: Pentagram Design; Partners in Charge: Colin Forbes, Michael Gericke; Designer: Donna Ching

Supporting Graphic Design: NON Associates

Illustrator: McRay Magleby

Interior Design: Intradesign

Project Art Direction and Management: Dentsu and OUN Design Corporation

Fabrication: Mercury Photo Engravers; Empire Plating & Polish

Photography: Robert Miller

Above left: The look is updated Art Nouveau. Floral images are popular in Japan, and the period Western style fits this international hotel.

Above right: Communicating the idea of luxury was a design objective. The identity was applied to signs, room folders, stationery, packaging, menus, and many other items.

Below: Each floor has its own floral symbol. The signs were made of metal to complement their opulent surroundings.

THE GOOD DINER

The designers were entrusted with naming this new New York City restaurant, as well as providing the graphics and consulting on the interior design. The client's objective was to offer simple food at a fair price, without being trendy or "retro."

Design: Pentagram Design; Partner/ Graphics: Michael Beirut; Partner/ Interior Design: James Biber; Partner/Illustrator: Woody Pirtle

Fabrication: ASI Sign Systems, Inc.; Manhattan Neon; Lane's Floor Coverings; Noris Metals; Awnings Unlimited

Photography: Reven T.C. Wurman

Left The logo, a cup of coffee "elevated to sainthood," appears everywhere — even inlaid in the linoleum floor.

Below left: Black and white striped awnings add dignity to a small outdoor dining space, while the front entrance is bright with practical — and fitting — neon signs.

Below right: The interior design celebrates ordinary diner materials, such as Naugahyde. Upholstered in a rainbow of colors, the seating perches under huge photocopies of simple diner objects: silverware, matchbooks, salt shakers.

SKYDOME

Home to the Blue Jays and the Argonauts, the 65,000-seat Toronto Skydome also hosts events of all descriptions. Its retractable roof inspired the bright identity graphics used on comprehensive wayfinding and advertising display programs.

Design: Gottschalk + Ash International and Keith Muller Associates Design Consortium

Gottschalk + Ash International: Partner: Stuart Ash; Design Team: Peter Adam, Brenda Tong, Robert Jensen, Kathe Wilcoxon, Katalin Kovats

Keith Muller Associates: Partner: Keith Muller; Design Team: Randy Johnson, Larry Burak, David Tonizzo, Joanna Crone, Robert Ketchen, Ian Watson

Client: Stadium Corporation of Ontario

Fabrication: King Products

Colorful banners featuring the sun, stars, rainbows and clouds — all visible inside because of the SkyDome's retractable roof — decorate the stadium. Giant, neon-trimmed gate signs help visitors find their entrance.

Inside, neon and painted graphics transform the otherwise utilitarian space.

Even the seats sport the SkyDome logo, which symbolizes the sky and the dome.

A comprehensive standards manual provides direction when using the identity program for new applications.

MIRAMAR SHERATON HOTEL

This magnificent gate includes a copper medallion with the hotel's street address inside a compass rose. Inside, a beautiful stone and metal compass flags a stone courtyard.

A new identity signals the Santa Monica, CA, hotel's renovation, and its change to five-star status. Signs, inspired by Frank Lloyd Wright's work, are made of elegant materials including copper, bronze, and laminated glass.

Design: Beck & Graboski Design Office; Principals: Constance Beck, Terry P. Graboski

Architecture: Solberg & Lowe Architects; DMJM Architects

Fabrication: AHR Ampersand; Windsor Displays; Cornelius Architectural Products; Wallach Glass Studio

Computerized Display: Morrow Technologies

Photography: Annette del Zoppo Productions: Jim Simmons; Terry P. Graboski

Opposite above: Meeting room signs feature etched laminated glass and LED displays connected to a central hotel computer.

Opposite below left: Inspired by Prairie style architecture, the directional signs are made of brushed copper and bronze, left without a topcoat so they will quickly age.

While the sign system doesn't skimp on technology, individual pieces are so finely made that some could be mistaken for antiques.

TURNING STONE CASINO

T he first legalized casino in New York state, Turning Stone is operated by the Oneida Indian Nation of New York and serves 10,000 visitors each day. A coordinated graphics and art program features gaming and Turning Stone themes.

Design: Chermayeff & Geismar, Inc.; Principal in Charge: Ivan Chermayeff; Designer: Daniela Perry

Client: Oneida Indian Nation of New York State

Walls: Dimensional Communications

Rock: Philip DiGacomo

Photography: Norman McGrath

Above left: At the entrance, a 20-ft. revolving cast stone turns once each minute. A similar, 12-ft. stone serves as the lobby centerpiece.

Above right: Curving casino walls are made to look like a deck of cards spread across a table. A custom alphabet and distinctive stone shapes decorate gaming tables, carpet, and souvenirs.

Left: The casino juice bar features glowing royal figures inspired by playing cards.

EMBARCADERO CENTER CINEMA NEON MURAL

A neon art mural for cinema buildings anchoring San Francisco's mixed-use Embarcadero Center presents a constantly changing pattern of color.

Design: Debra Nichols Design; Project Manager: Bill Comstock

Client: Pacific Properties

Fabrication: Superior Signs

Photography: Chas McGrath

The computer-controlled system changes the illuminated pattern every 30 seconds. It's programmed for different sequences at different times of day, to match the area's changing pace and activities.

Five different complete programs run on different days, so that viewers never see the same thing two days in a row.

SAN JOSE ARENA

This complete graphic package includes all signs, stores and concession stands, food carts, architectural consultation, press materials and marketing, and uniform designs. The result is a complete and distinctive look with a sense of fun.

Design: The Office of Michael Manwaring; Project Designer: Michael Manwaring; Designer: Jeff Inouye

Client: San Jose Redevelopment Agency

Fabrication: Heath & Co., (prime signage contractor)

Photography: Michael Manwaring, Jeff Inouye

Seen in context, the giant letters and symbols barely avoid being dwarfed by the building's scale.

Above: Even signs for automobiles, often given no design attention or construction budget, match the arena's look. The visitors' experience of "place" does not begin in the parking lot elevator or stadium door, but long before they leave their cars.

Below left: Finding rooms in vast stadiums and arenas can be difficult. Here, the designers made it easy with giant striped symbols — letters over restrooms, arrows over elevators — perched on top of common destinations.

Below right: Striped pylons ringing the arena feature stylized torches.

GUND ARENA

What began as an identity and sign commission for this Cleveland, OH, arena turned into a complete identity package including consulting on interior design, retail and restaurant work, and even uniforms. Design was inspired by the city's industrial past, as well as by the sports and performances taking place inside the arena.

Design: Sussman/Prejza & Co., Inc.; Principal: Deborah Sussman; Associate in Charge: Mark Nelsen; Interiors Architect: Fernando Vazquez; Designers:Paul Novacek, Dan Evans, Lance Glover, Charles Milhaupt, Billy Rosbottom, John Johnston

Client: Gund Investment Corporation; Gateway Economic Development Corporation of Greater Cleveland

Fabrication/Consultants: Carlson + Co.; Architectural Graphics Inc.(AGI)

Photography: Timothy Hursley; Mark Nelsen

Customers can follow the game with both closed-circuit television and an updating scoreboard while at this snack bar.

The designers consulted on much of the interior design, including this restaurant.

This lounge incorporates a football motif in both the yard-marker floor graphics as well as the football-shaped booth.

CAESAR'S MAGICAL EMPIRE

This subterranean Las Vegas attraction looks as if it's been untouched for 2,000 years. Polished marble in the ticket area gives way to decayed and cracked plaster over hand-carved block walls (in the Catacomb Maze) and even large rock formations (in the Sanctum Secorum). Playful "classical" signs keep up the lighthearted fun.

Design: Landmark Entertainment Group

Client: Caesar's Palace

Fabrication: Signtech Seattle

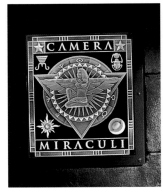

Ancient symbols and modern materials mark this sign for the Chamber of Miracles.

Chariots of the Gods? Even the access signs get into the act.

An impressive, classical-style monument serves as the entrance and ticket booth for Caesar's Magical Empire, which features "grand scale illusions" as well as fine dining.

Above: The rough stone walls and Egyptian carvings of the Forbidden Crypt promise a delightfully frightening experience.

Below left: Restroom signs for the sighted may be marked "uomini," but the blind — unable to see the sculpture — read "men."

Below right: The mysteries of the East are not forgotten in Caesar's Magical Empire.

THE TROCADERO

C ombining leading-edge technology with a "hyper-charged commercial environment," the almost-indescribable Trocadero exudes energy. Animatronic graphics are only one of the many highlights of this attraction in London's Piccadilly Circus.

Design: RTKL Associates, Inc.; Project Manager: David Gester; Design Team: Paul G. Hanegraaf, Thom McKay, Glyn Rees, Chris Jones, Tim Baker

Client: Burford Group PC

Show Consultant: Media Projects

Audio Visual: Vincent Rice Design

Lighting Consultant: Jonathan Speirs

Neon Sign Fabrication: Oldham Signs

Sign Fabrication: Butterfield Signs

Photography: David Whitcomb, RTKL

Reflective metal sheeting and video displays add to the vibrant atmosphere.

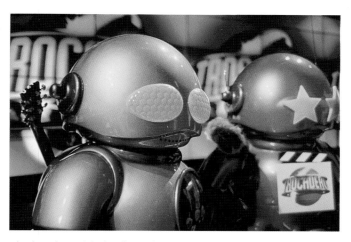

Like the robot sidekicks of countless B movies, animatronic figures are part of the action.

Futuristic neon-clad columns and escalators surround visitors with light and graphics.

BRING IN 'DA NOISE, BRING IN 'DA FUNK MURALS

A smash hit at The Public Theater, New York City, this musical history of rhythm in African-American life is also famous for its graphics. Designed in the wood-type style featured on all Public Theater graphics, the show's advertising signs feature photos of dancer/choreographer Savion Glover.

Design: Pentagram Design; Designers: Paula Scher, Lisa Mazur

Client: The Public Theater

Dancer Photography: Richard Avedon, Peter Harrison, Carol Rosegg, Eduardo Patino

Documentation Photography: Peter Margonelli, Kurt Koepfle, Matt Petosa

"Bring in 'Da Noise, Bring in 'Da Funk" is only one of many Public Theater productions, which include its famous Shakespeare in the Park. Here choreographer/dancer Savion Glover challenges passers-by to see his show.

The versatile graphics adapt to all shapes and sizes, and all materials — including this vehicle graphic and even chalk on pavement.

Left: Giant feet walk over the New York streets on this giant sign.

Below: Wood type and old-fashioned poster design mark the Public Theater's new artistic direction, streetwise and accessible.

SECTION 4
RETAIL AND SERVICE ENVIRONMENTS

Levi's Jeans for Women Shop

Year after year, people become more accustomed to good design. They have begun to expect it and, increasingly, demand it in the places they visit to shop and relax. In the United States, this design awareness is largely due to ever-higher standards in retail and entertainment graphics. They set the standards for others to meet or exceed.

A/X: Armani Exchange

Apple Exhibit Expansion Program

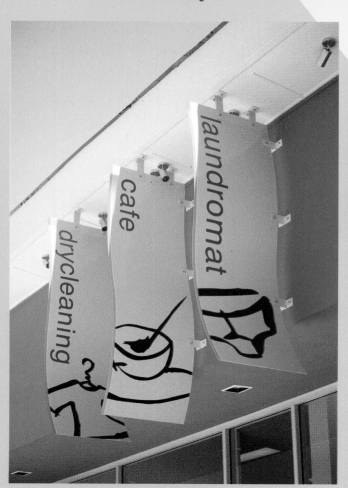

Hang-Out Laundry Dry Cleaning, Sydney, Australia

Instead of typical horizontal shelves and light box displays, this exhibit contained a number of rooms devoted to different functions. Displays included freestanding units for new books, racks for finished proofs, shelves for dummies, and "spine-out" displays for backlist titles.

Design: Gee + Chung Design;
Designer: Earl Gee

Client: Chronicle Books

Fabrication: Barr Exhibits

Photography: Andy Caulfield

Left: Innovative displays included "stairstep" shelves and bars for hanging calendars. The carpentry and construction imagery symbolize the client's commitment to work and progress.

Below: This giant trade show display invited visitors to browse different rooms, each devoted to a different function.

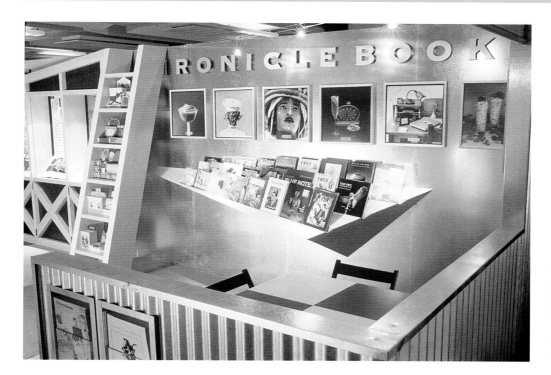

Cozy corners invited visitors to sit and look at finished proofs of new books.

THE CITADEL

T his mixed-use center in City of Commerce, CA, takes its name from the site, a fantastical building that was once the largest tire factory on the U.S. West Coast. Graphics and new architecture explore a combination of low-tech industrial elements and Hollywood fantasy.

Design: Sussman/Prejza & Co. Inc.; Principal-in-Charge and Creative Director: Deborah Sussman; Senior Designer: Holly Hampton; Project Manager of Signage and Graphics: Scott Cuyler; Project Manager of Retail Architectural Design: Fernando Vazquez

Client: Trammel

Fabrication: Ad Art/Signs Inc., Heath Sign Company

The sign for the center's outlet stores towers high above in industrial-style splendor.

The Citadel's graphics are inspired by the site's original building, a tire factory built in a fantasy Assyrian style.

Below left: Signs explore both Hollywood myth and industrial reality. Here tires crown the brightly colored, industrial-style directory.

Below right: The signature Assyrian gryphon appears on signs. Giant "tires" surround palm trees in the innovative landscaping.

BMW EXHIBIT

F our cars displayed on two "overpasses" made visual impact in this 1,200-sq.-ft. trade show exhibit at the 1993 International Auto Show in Detroit. Behind the mirrored curtain wall, a two-level structure housed a VIP lounge and executive office.

Design: Interbrand Corporation; Project Designer/Manager: Roger Sonanini
Fabrication: General Exhibits & Displays
Photography: Felix Streuli

Two curving "overpasses" displayed four BMW vehicles high above the heads of the crowd, utilizing vertical space and providing a visual focal point.

Right: Interactive touch screens and real BMW engines gave visitors a close-up look at the cars.

Below: New vehicles were displayed on two turntables. Interpretive signs and interactive video kiosks gave visitors in-depth information about the company and products. The mirrored wall hid a two-level structure housing a VIP lounge and an office.

YOU ARE HERE: GRAPHICS THAT DIRECT, EXPLAIN & ENTERTAIN

HERMAN MILLER DISTRIBUTION EXHIBITION

T his 130-ft. wall at Herman Miller's Distribution Center in Zeeland, MI, introduces visitors to the company. It includes a historical timeline and an explanation of how orders are handled, from the initial phone call to the packing, loading, and shipping.

Design: Carol Naughton & Associates Inc.; Designers: Carol Naughton, Daniel Morgenthaler, Edward Kuliesis

Fabrication: Paul Idec

Photographs, diagrams, packing crates, and even painted tire marks illustrate delivery.

Left: Interpretive graphics begin with a map of the facility, followed by a timeline of the company's history illustrated with photographs and documents.

Below: Graphics are not confined to two-dimensional displays. Artifacts help bring the exhibit to life.

JOHN DEERE DEALER MEETING

A laser show was the highlight of this meeting for John Deere dealers in Maimarkthalle, Mannheim, Germany. Instead of traditional construction, funds went toward what planners felt would best motivate dealers.

A laser show provided drama and excitement to the dealer meeting, highlighting new products in a memorable way.

Right: Instead of traditional construction, lighting transformed the room and provided drama. Custom fabric banners added a tactile dimension.

Below right: Light and fabric also transformed the meeting's theater space.

Design: Group/Chicago, Inc.;
Principal in Charge/Designer: Kurt Meinecke
Client: John Deere & Co., Mannheim, Germany

Producer: Don Manelli & Associates

Lighting: Upstaging/Chameleon

Laser Show: Lasertech

Fabric Design: Transformit

Fabrication: Proto Productions

Photography: Mike Christian

JBL ON-BOARD

hree related but distinct demonstration areas fit into one cohesive whole at this booth for the 1994 Comdex show in Las Vegas. An existing eight-person sound room, a surround-sound area, and an arcade of multimedia podiums introduced JBL's presence in the emerging personal entertainment industry.

Design: Fitch Inc.; Vice Presidents: Ann Gildea and Michael Mooney; Program Manager and Associate Vice President: Jane Brady; Associate Vice President: Mark Steele; Senior Associates: Christian Uhland, Ben Segal

Client: JBL Consumer Products

Fabrication: Farmington Displays, Inc.

Photography: Aperture

Simple materials and spare design give the exhibit quiet elegance. Large walls act as a canvas for evocative type.

Left: Three separate product demonstration areas were housed in one cohesive exhibit. Here, the eight-person sound room does duty as a "cinema."

Below: Multimedia "podiums" allowed visitors to try out products.

Intel's objectives for this telecommunications trade show in Geneva, the world's largest and most prestigious, were to position the company as a world leader and to bring international customers together.

Design: George P. Johnson Co.; Design Manager: Jeff Bartle; Project designer: Mike Taran

Client: Intel

Fabrication: Andreas Messerli

Photography: Michel Zumbrunn

Giant shapes and glowing letters made an impression on the trade show floor.

Rooms allowed for small
meetings and product
demonstrations.

A/X: ARMANI EXCHANGE

Beyond designing a new store for New York City, this project also included creating a logo for Armani jeans, retail signing, and package design.

Design: Alexander Isley Inc.; Art Director: Alexander Isley; Designers: Alexander Knowlton, Bruno Nesci, Tim Convery

Created in Association with: Weiss, Whiteen Carroll, Stagliano Advertising

Client: Giorgio Armani

Architect: Naomi Leff & Associates

Fabrication: Christopher Vincent Inc.; Akron Metal Etching Co.

Photography: Peter Paige

Right: The store's spare, Japanese look highlights the casual but classic clothes.

Below left: Signs, graphics, and package design all work together to create a consistent, evocative look for a new store.

Below right: A clean, easy-to-read chart guides customers among many choices in Armani jeans.

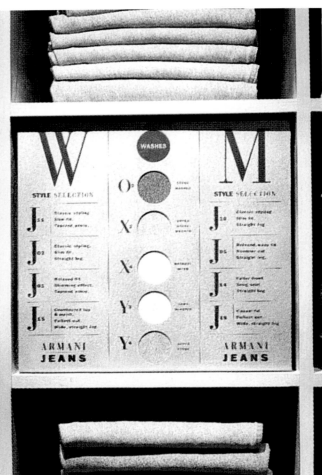

DUNCAN AVIATION TRADESHOW EXHIBIT

T his exhibit for a full-service business jet maintenance company provided an environment for meeting with current and potential customers. Its style was meant to communicate the company's values.

Clocks reinforced the company's claims at expertise in "time management."

Left: The exhibit's elegant and expensive look reflected the company's business and clientele, and also fit the trade show — a high-tech extravaganza in which airplane manufacturers show their new planes.

Below: Black and white portraits of employees made the exhibit more personal, and focused on the company's promise of excellent service.

Design: Mauk Design; Creative Director: Mitchell Mauk; Designer: Adam Brodsley

Client: Duncan Aviation

Fabrication: Ironwind

Portrait Photographer: Robert Wilken

Exhibit Photographer: Paul Bowen

Photography: Andy Caulfield

C omputer exhibits typically last three to five years. At eight, Apple's system was still going strong. But its extreme flexibility meant huge costs in design, setup, teardown, and refurbishing. The new, simplified design extended the system's life by five years while reusing $7 million worth of parts.

Design: Mauk Design; Creative Director: Mitchell Mauk; Designers: Tim Mautz, Adam Brodsley

Client: Apple Computer

Original Mainframe Design: Paul Segal

Fabrication/Design: General Exhibits & Displays

Photography: Julie Chase

The redesign saved Apple $7 million in parts, while eliminating all but the top-performing elements. The resulting lean look captures the company's current advertising style.

Before

The eight-year-old Apple exhibit system, Mainframe, had become cluttered and out-of-date. The extruded aluminum system saved money in fabrication, but its many complex parts cost large sums for each design, setup, and teardown.

Fabric panels, printed subtly with faces of Apple users, cover the modular frame.

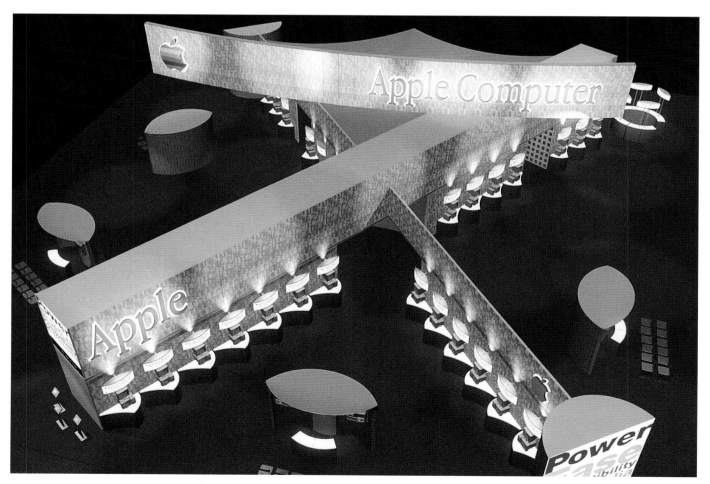

SONY PLAZA, INC.

A series of spaces including retail stores, restaurants, and a four-story interactive museum, Sony Plaza in New York City was a new retail venture for Sony. Designers created two retail stores designed around "event islands" presenting the range of Sony products. They also designed the commissary and public atrium.

The new Sony headquarters piles offices with windows high above giant "doors" and "windows" that are, in part, the setting for the company's new retail venture.

Huge banners lining the public atrium introduce the various shops and restaurants.

Designers filled the vast spaces with light, sound and movement.

A "beam" of light and Sony's logo projected on walls lead shoppers through the complicated spaces of this store.

Design: Edwin Schlossberg, Inc.; Principal Designer: Edwin Schlossberg; Project Manager: Diane Klein; Project Designer: Kim Jennings; Graphic designer: Joseph Mayer; Technical Designer: Dean Markosian

Client: Sony Corporation of America

Fabrication: Rathe Productions

Lighting: Don Holder and Maggie Giusto Lighting Design

Photography: Donald Dietz

Left: An array of products of all types inundates the visitor with purchasing choices.

Below: The facade of the Sony Commissary beckons with a quiet, classic look.

HANG-OUT LAUNDRY DRY CLEANING

T he same designers created all graphics, interiors, signs, and merchandise for this "new concept in clean clothes" in Sydney, Australia. Fun graphics convince people to come in and "hang out."

Design: Ashdown Wood Design Consultants Pty, Ltd.; Design Director: Jan Ashdown; Interior Designer: Kelvin Murray; Signage and Graphics Designer: Phillippa Carnemolla; Project Manager: Bill Ward

Client: Hang Out Pty, Ltd.

Fabrication: Cunneen & Co.

Project Builder: Wee Datum

Vertical signs curve to recall laundry hanging from a line.

Left: The simple interior boasts clean lines as well as clean clothes.

Below left: Branded merchandise reinforces the idea that Hang Out is a fun place to go, not a necessary-but-unpleasant stop-off.

Below right: Interior signs continue the carefree graphics.

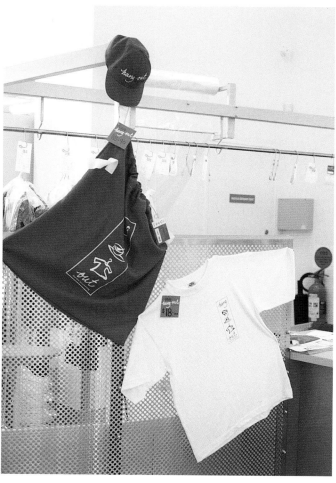

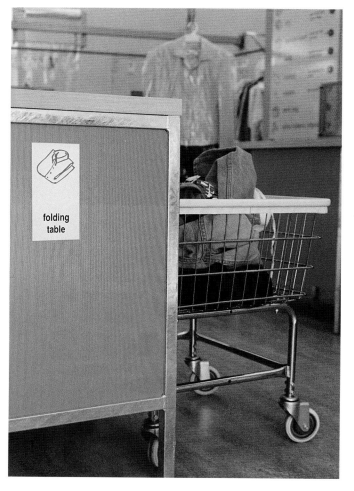

"CORIAN? CORIAN!" TRADE SHOW EXHIBIT

Best known as a material used to make countertops, Corian needed to make a splash with interior designers. For this exhibit at the International Contemporary Furniture Fair in New York City, designers showed Corian's untapped potential in curved, colored walls, furniture, and textures. The object was to make designers ask, "Corian?" and to answer, "Corian!"

Design: Pentagram Design; Partner-in-Charge/Architect: James Biber; Associate/Architect: Michael Zweck-Bronner; Graphic Designer: Nicole Richardson; Project Coordinator: Leslie Wellott

Client: DuPont Corian

Fabrication: Art Guild

Photography: Peter Margonelli

Backlighting also demonstrated Corian's translucency, more untapped potential for designers to use.

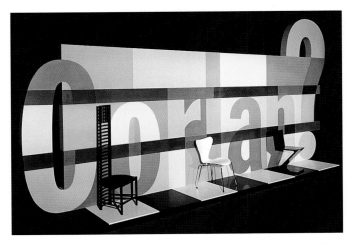

A freestanding wall made of Corian, in a new color palette designed by Pentagram, stood next to reproductions of famous furniture designs — also rendered in Corian.

A second wall, perpendicular to the first, was made of white and off-white Corian. Dramatically backlit, it showcased how the material responded to routing, sandblasting, and carving.

STRIDE RITE STORES

More that a store redesign, this new identity unified Stride Rite — from wholesale catalogues to merchandising systems for independent distributors. Multicultural and gender-equal designs focus on the joy of growing up.

Design: Selbert Perkins Design Collaborative; Design Team: Robin Perkins, Clifford Selbert, Michele Phelan, Julia Daggett, Kamren Colson, Kim Reese, John Lutz

Client: Stride Rite Corp.

Consultants: Design Communications; GF&T + Co.; Elkus/Manfredi Architects Ltd.

Illustrator: Gerald Bustamante

Photography: Jim Webber, Anton Grassl

Interior graphics feature photographs of happy children. Written messages emphasize the company's reputation for quality and its understanding of fun children's fashions.

Two happy faces, which can be seen as a boy and a girl of different races, form the essence of the logo. Though gender-equal and multicultural, the design can't be accused of losing any of its fresh charm to political correctness.

Merchandising works well in both distributor stores and Stride Rite stores.

Custom fixtures, furniture, and carpeting help give this 3,200-sq.-ft., in-store shop its unique character. All design is based on the theme of a woman's curving shape. Writing, which appears on the carpets and on dress forms, is based on entries from a woman's journal.

Design: Morla Design; Creative Director: Brian Collins, Foote Cone + Belding; Art Directors: Jennifer Morla and Eric Rindal, Foote Cone + Belding; Designer: Jennifer Morla

Copywriter: Suzanne Finnamore

Fixtures and Furniture: Fun Display; Mobius Inc.

Carpeting: Bentley Carpets

Photography: Sheila Metzner

Sensuous photographic murals emphasize the shape of women's bodies, while the dress forms placed throughout the space are in different body sizes. Both suggest that Levi's clothes are designed to fit real women.

The design for the in-store shop at Macy's department store in New York City, is based on a woman's shape. Custom furnishings and fixtures set the tone, while words inspired by a woman's journal flow across the custom carpeting and dress forms.

DAVID JONES DEPARTMENT STORE

These temporary, celebratory graphics painted the "face" of one of Sydney, Australia's most famous landmarks, the David Jones department store. Always considered friendly and personal, the store is famous for serving "the women of Sydney." Giant photos of 134 Sydney women, including the store's eldest customer, 101-year-old Miss Edith Whitlock, covered every window.

Design: Cato Design Inc.; Principal in Charge: Ken Cato

Fabrication: 3M Australia

In a striking, celebratory design, photos of 134 Sydney women covered every window of the famed David Jones department store in Sydney, Australia.

Photos, both color and black and white, ranged in size. Some took up only one window, some covered three or four stories.

INTEL SIGGRAPH EXHIBIT

This hip exhibit was designed to help Intel overcome its stodgy image and appeal to a twentysomething crowd of film and computer video animators. To attract this lucrative market, Intel's exhibit featured giant "Polygon People," demo videos shown in internally illuminated fiberglass orbs, a giant video wall, and live performers. Most of the materials are recyclable and all are reusable.

Design: Mauk Design; Creative Director: Mitchell Mauk; Designers: Adam Brodsley, Laurence Raines, Mitchell Mauk

Consultants: Live Marketing

Fabrication: Exhibitgroup/Giltspur

Photography: Andy Caulfield

Giant "Polygon People," human forms reduced to their basic shapes for computer animation, lined the Intel exhibit. Made of plasma-cut, quarter-in. aluminum, the five male and five female figures were shown "moving" from standing to running, to emphasize the Intel platform's speed.

Instead of running in the background, Intel's video wall was an integral part of its live presentation. The stage split in two, and attendees followed the presenter "inside" to the demonstration area.

The "Pentium II Dancers" had people dancing in the aisles, part of a successful effort to get the client noticed by a new market.

Below: Attendees could view demo tapes on 27-in. monitors inside internally illuminated fiberglass "orbs" (seen from above). Because this exhibit qualified as a multiple-story building, much of the project's $600,000 budget was spent on meeting stringent Los Angeles building codes.

One demonstration area and its "orb."

HANLEY-WOOD TRADE SHOW EXHIBIT

The client, an architectural and construction magazine publisher, wanted a high-end design that nevertheless connected it to the "industry." A combination of industrial materials and lights, together with stylish curved walls and "ceilings," was the result. Oversized, color reproductions of magazine covers were displayed in a surprising, dramatic way.

Design: McMillan Group, Inc.; Principal in Charge: Charlie McMillan; Designers: Charlie McMillan, Patrick McCauley, John Grasso

Fabrication: IDEAS

Consultants: Jamie Padgett, Padgett and Co.

This tradeshow exhibit for a magazine publisher combined industrial materials with sophisticated design. Curved walls and overhead wings gave the space an Oriental look.

The centerpiece conference room was framed by curving, black-framed shoji screens. A distinctive table finished the look.

Giant color reproductions of magazine covers speared through the curved "wings," displaying the client's product in an innovative way.

Two McDonald's restaurants in two states received a new design treatment integrating architecture, graphics and space. The corporate identity is expressed throughout both, as part of the interior and exterior architecture.

Design: Gensler; Graphic Design: Jane Brady, Dian Duvall, Julie Tashima, Lisa Van Zandt; Architecture Design: Kevin Hart, John Ishihara, Jean Lavan, Andrew Meagher; Retail Design: Michael Bodziner, Dana Frost, Jeff Henry, Julie Lochowski-Haney, Suzanne Korock, Katie Price; Principal-in-Charge: Charlie Kridler

Consultant: Frankel & Co.

Fabrication: Expo Trans; Frankel & Co.; Florida Plastics; Hollywood Outdoor Advertising; JBI; Plasti-Line Inc.; YESCO

Photography: Nora Scarlett and Chris Barrett, Hedrich Blessing Photographers; Chris Seager, Gensler

Like a beacon, a giant box of french fries at the Colorado Springs store beckons customers. Larger than the "golden arches" sign outside, it is both sign and sculpture.

Inside the Colorado Springs store, menu graphics become part of the decor. Instead of squinting to see one giant menu board over the clerks' heads, patrons can look at the small menu board posted by each cash register.

At the Darien, IL, store, illuminated golden arches function as a brand-reinforcing room divider.

BLOCKBUSTER MUSIC

Light, video, and undulating walls bring movement to music display, traditionally a static design.

A concept store for Blockbuster Entertainment, Blockbuster Music in Ft. Lauderdale, FL, looks far different from traditional music stores. Its objective was to move beyond movie rentals into other family entertainment businesses.

Design: Fitch Inc.; Senior Vice President: Matthew Napoleon; Vice Presidents: Paul Lechleiter, Mark Artus, Beth Dorsey; Senior Associates: Maribeth Gatchalian, Scott Richardson; Directors: Paul Harlorr, Alycia Freeman, Kian Kuan, Joanie Hupp; Associate Vice Presidents: Sandy McKissick, Mark Steele

Client: Blockbuster Entertainment

Fabrication: Art Sign Company; BSG Industries, Inc.; California Neon Products; Chandler Signs; Chroma Studios; Excell Store Fixtures, Inc.; Falkenger Architects; Ford Audio Video; Gisondi Painting and Wallcovering, Inc.; Gopher Products; Lighting Management, Inc.; Rodgers Wade; SGI, Texas; Wyko-Mica Products

Photography: Fitch Inc.

Separate "stores," each with sampling areas, cater to fans of different music types.

Even the displays carried on the design's focus on light and shadow.

SECTION 5
URBAN AND TEMPORARY ENVIRONMENTS

Houston Uptown Streetscape

Graphics in urban environments solve the same problems tackled in other projects, with one major difference. Scale. Even the largest hospital campus or stadium is dwarfed by almost any urban project. Designers taking on such projects must learn to look at environmental graphics a whole new way. The size, distances, and numbers of people affected make urban projects especially challenging. Also difficult are temporary signs and environmental graphics, which though not permanent, must be as equally effective.

UnversityCenter, Baltimore

Japanese American Historical Plaza, Portland

Denver Children's Museum 20th Anniversary

THE CLIFFS BOARDWALK

Distinctive signs have the river's bend cut into their metal faces.

Undulating paving patterns help bring the pedestrian and bicycle path a distinctive look.

This two-kilometer pedestrian and cycle path along the Brisbane River in Queensland, Australia, winds through urban development and a historic quarry. Designers created signs, maps, tiling patterns for viewing platforms, and pedestrian crossings. They also found and installed a sculpture series last seen at World Expo 88 (hosted by Brisbane), giving it new life and purpose.

Design: Dot Dash; Designer: Mark Ross; Artist: Peter D. Cole; Structural Engineer: Roderick Bligh

Architecture/Project Manager: Q Build Project Services

Photography: Linkins Photographers

A group of dancing metal figures is part of "Man and Matter," a 14-piece sculpture series created by Peter D. Cole for the 1988 World Expo. In storage since the fair, the series was refurbished and given a new, permanent life along the river.

The playful spirit of Cole's sculptures adds a delightful visual element to the Cliffs Boardwalk, integrating art with leisure.

PATH UNDERGROUND WALKWAY

The largest pedestrian network of its kind in North America, Path links Toronto, Canada, transit and commuter systems with indoor concourses. It runs through hundreds of stores, restaurants and entertainment centers, and provides access to the city's commercial and financial services.

Design: Gottschalk + Ash International/Keith Muller Associates

Gottschalk + Ash International: Principal: Stuart Ash; Design Team: Diane Castellan, Katalin Kovats

Keith Muller Associates: Principal: Keith Muller; Design Team: Randy Johnson, Merritt Price

Client: City of Toronto

Fabrication: King Products

The four squares unite numerous sign types and sizes.

A sample sign shows the program's symbol: the word "path" in four letter styles, each of the letters a separate square.

Quality workmanship is important to the system's overall look.

DIRECTION PHILADELPHIA

Guidelines spell out the system's distinct look, which includes typefaces, decorative motifs, sign types, distinctive fabrication specifications, and a palette of bright colors.

T his citywide vehicular sign program directs drivers from highways to downtown sites. A hierarchy of sign types makes district identification, parking facilities, directional signs, and highway trailblazers easy to identify and understand. The designers also created a separate, but related, system for Fairmont Park.

Design: Sussman/Prejza & Co.; Principal in Charge: Paul Prejza; Associate in Charge: Debra Valencia; Design Team: Tom Carr, Jennifer Bass, Corky Retson

Client: Foundation for Architecture and The City of Philadelphia

Fabrication: Adelphia Graphic Systems (ADG), Architectural Graphics Inc.(AGI)

Consultants: Kise, Franks & Straw, Newbold's/American Capital Group, The Busch Center of the Wharton School, Montgomery McCracken Walker & Rhodes, Leslie Gallery-Dilworth

Photography: J.B. Abbott

Equally at home amid skyscrapers and pre-Revolution buildings, the sign system fits its home.

Even the sign backs are distinctive and well crafted.

BATTERY PARK PARKS

T hese graphics identify and beautify a series of 25 parks enclosing Battery Park City, a community at the southern tip of New York's Manhattan Island. Begun in 1988, the continuing project visually unifies the neighborhood. Super-durable materials, such as porcelain enamel, were chosen to stand up to the use and abuse of park visitors, many of whom do not restrain their large dogs.

Design: Sales from Design; Principal in Charge: Julie Salestrom

Client: Battery Park City Authority & Parks Corp.

Fabrication: King Products, Enameltec, Pioneer Porcelain, Letterama, Signs & Decal

Thick metal poles and porcelain enamel panels are meant to withstand hard use from, among others, children and dogs. The graphic emblem of the system is the metal hoop shape, taken from the fences around flower beds.

Print collateral shows the project identity, featuring the metal hoop fences used on flower beds in the park.

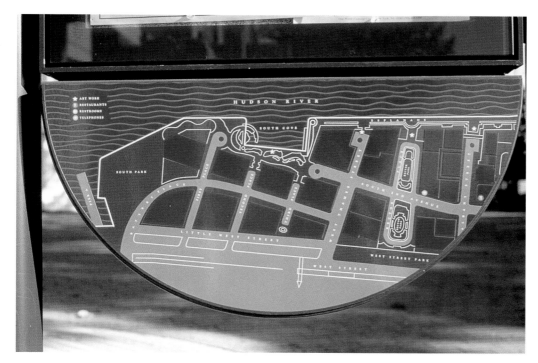

These bulletin board signs also include durable maps, which show landmarks rather than changeable attractions.

D eveloped over four years, this comprehensive system helps humanize the a 1.1 million-sq.-ft. space at the Chicago airport. It covers 21 gates, a ticketing pavilion, support facilities, administrative offices, a transit station, baggage claim areas, recheck facilities and Federal Inspection Services (FIS) areas.

Design: Carol Naughton & Associates, Inc.; Principal in Charge: Carol Naughton; Designers: Kim Cardosi, Vick Moore, Edward Kuliesis

Client: Department of Aviation, City of Chicago

Fabrication: Whiteway Signs

Photography: Vick Moore, Hedrich Blessing

International-style graphics make the soaring architecture and cavernous spaces intelligible to users from around the world.

Below left: The ticketing area alone requires scores of signs.

Above: Programmable LED signs in the FIS area can display information in 18 languages.

This tiny plaza along Portland's riverfront tells a big story: the internment of Japanese Americans during World War II.

A waterfront park and memorial to the more than 110,000 Japanese American citizens interned in camps during WWII, this plaza along a Portland, OR, riverfront is also a tribute to the Bill of Rights. A curving basalt and granite wall tells the story. The Bill of Rights anchors the south end of the wall; the Congressional Apology of 1988 the north.

Design: Anderson Krygier, Inc.; Principal in Charge: Elizabeth Anderson; Designer: John Krygier

Client: Oregon Nikkei Foundation, Portland, OR

Landscape Architect: Murase Associates

Poetry: Lawson Inada, Hisako Saito, Shizue Iwatsuki, Masatoshi Izumi

Sculpture: Jim Gion

Fabrication: Harmax Bronze (Macadam Aluminum and Bronze Foundry), Vancouver Granite Works

Photography: John Krygier, Robert Murase

Above: Poetry in two languages tells Japanese-American stories. The carefully placed stones recall Japanese gardens.

Below: Cherry trees add more Japanese-American symbolism. The complete texts of important American legislation relating to the internment are reproduced on bronze plaques.

HOUSTON UPTOWN STREETSCAPE

A mbitious new signs, street furniture, landscaping and art give a new public image to a special tax district in Houston. Businesses raised their taxes to pay for the improvements.

Design: Communication Arts, Inc.; Design Principal: Henry Beer; Project Manager: Leonard Thomas; Designers: Mike Doyle, Bryan Gough; Project Director: John Ward

Client: Harris County Improvement District #1, Houston

Architecture: Sikes, Jennings, Radley & Brewster

Fabrication: Offenhauser Company; Milestone Metals, Inc.; Intex United, Inc.; Neon Electric Corporation; Union Metal

Consultants: Walter P. Moore & Associates, engineers; Slaney Santana Group, landscape architects

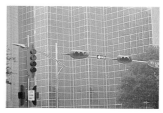

Above left: Giant stainless steel arcs cross the highway in pairs, uniting tiny "pocket parks" on either side of the road.

Above right: New light poles and other structures give the street a distinctive look.

Below: Internally illuminated, stainless steel disks hover over intersections.

UNIVERSITYCENTER

A newly named district in the heart of Baltimore, UniversityCenter includes numerous medical centers and the Ridgely's Delight neighborhood. Graphics had to overcome the area's negative image and create visual character. Inspired by the state's new plan to promote excellence in the life sciences, designers based their work on the area's medical research facilities.

Design: Cloud and Gehshan Associates, Inc.; Principal in Charge/Concept: Virginia Gehshan; Design Director: Jerome Cloud; *Design Team:* Jerome Cloud, Ann McDonald

Client: UniversityCenter

Landscape Architects: Wallace Roberts & Todd

Fabrication: Nordquist Sign Co., Inc.

Photography: Tom Crane

Graphics give character to the newly named neighborhood, formerly an amorphous group of streets with no identity. A double helix, symbolizing DNA molecules, and the motto "Neighborhood of Discovery" tie together a number of different sign types.

Maps show the neighborhood's boundaries and reveal its assets.

The graphics program has given the neighborhood new vitality, and has been adopted by many University of Maryland divisions.

EMBARCADERO HISTORICAL AND INTERPRETIVE SIGNAGE

A public arts project along two and a half miles of the San Francisco waterfront, this interpretive graphics project includes porcelain enamel pylons, cast concrete podiums, and bronze plaques embedded in the sidewalk.

Design: The Office of Michael Manwaring; Project Designer: Michael Manwaring; Design Team: Elizabeth Ives Manwaring, Tim Perks

Client: The San Francisco Art Commission; Director of Public Art Programs: Jill Manton

Fabrication: Thomas Swan Sign Co.; General Graphics; Fireform Porcelain Inc.; South Bay Bronze

Historian and Writer: Nancy Leigh Olmstead

Poetry, prose, and more conventional interpretive text work with photographs and graphics to make the area's past visible.

Cast concrete podiums with porcelain enamel panels make another distinctive mark on the San Francisco streetscape.

Porcelain enamel pylons present area history and natural history in an innovative way.

T he National Park Service made it easy for little towns along a 95-mile "corridor" to acquire great signs by hiring designers to create detailed guidelines for them to adopt and implement. The goal is to give the towns a uniform but custom look and direct people to their attractions.

Design: Cloud and Gehshan Associates, Inc.: Principal in Charge/Design Director: Jerome Cloud; Design Team: Jerome Cloud, Cheryl Hanba, Margo Borten Reardon, Thomas Corlett

Client: United States Department of the Interior/National Park Service

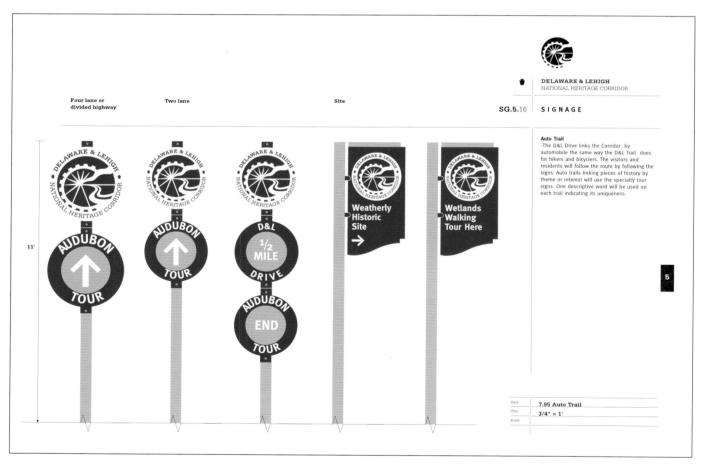

Detailed design and fabrication specifications allow even the most inexperienced to choose and order signs.

Guidelines include specifications for interpretive signs, such as this one built for Easton, PA.

A directional sign for Easton, PA, was one of the first signs in the program to be implemented.

NORTH PARK COMMUNITY IMPROVEMENTS

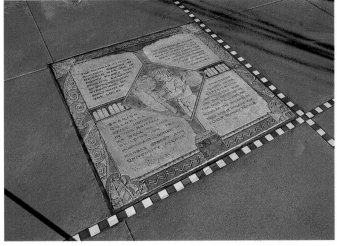

Tiles set into colored pavement explain area history.

This streetscape enhancement program was designed to meet strict federal Main Street standards, combining an area's history with contemporary design and materials. The project includes sidewalk enhancements, bus shelters and seating, and an identity gateway.

Design: Wieber Nelson Design; Principal in Charge: Harmon O. Nelson III

Consultant: Carol Kerr Graphic Design

Fabrication: California Neon Products; Progressive Concrete

Photography: Mike Campos

Above left: Fanciful bus seating also provides shelter in the rain. The project, built with federal Main Street funds, also included a community gateway sign.

Above right: Brilliant neon lights the gateway sign and bus shelters at night.

HERITAGE TRAILS NEW YORK

"Tourists" can preview the four trails and plan their days at information kiosks, where they can use interactive videos and get trail guides.

F our walking tours through Downtown Manhattan link 50 historic and contemporary sites with freestanding interpretive graphic panels. Colored dots set into the pavement and hand-held maps are wayfinding aids. Visitors can plan their days and preview their tours at interactive video kiosks

Design: Chermayeff & Geismar Inc.; Project Designer/Manager: Keith Helmetag; Partner Input: Ivan Chermayeff, John Grady; Designers: Anthony Ferrara, Alex Yampolsky; Production: Charlotte Noruzi

Fabrication: Ariston

Photography: Karen Yamauchi

Interpretive graphics explain sites with words and photos.

Trail guidebooks contain maps, photographs, and information about the 50 sites. Each trail is color-coded. Colored dots, marked with the Heritage Trail logo and set into the pavement, mark trails.

T his installation for a Skid Row shelter in Los Angeles dignifies and empowers a largely invisible community. Two related elements — the "Orientation Rotunda" and the "Electronic Statement" — present and preserve the words of homeless men.

Design: BJ Krivanek Art + Design; Design Director: BJ Krivanek; Designer: Joel Breaux; Technical Assistant: Martha Najera

Client: National Endowment for the Arts, The Los Angeles Endowment for the Arts

Fabrication: Peter Carlson Enterprises

Photography: Jeff Kurt Petersen

An electronic sign on the building's exterior presents a never-ending stream of words.

Left: The illuminated dome in the shelter's rotunda contrasts words describing positive and negative male qualities.

Below: Murals further explore the gap between what homeless men might desire to be with what their lives have become.

T he construction hoarding, or barricade, introduced the public to a large federal reconstruction project covering 16 Vancouver sites for veteran's housing. A prototype for similar programs throughout Canada, it involved the area by serving as a community notice board.

Design: PUBLIK Information Design; Design Director/Designer: Arlene Cotter; Illustrators: Steve Van Gelder, Si Huynh/Rep Art; Writers: Arlene Cotter, Gary Hiscox

Client: Canada Mortgage & Housing Corporation, Kitsilano Project

Fabrication: Clay Signs

Photography: Peter Timmermans

Information-rich text included maps and other project specifics.

Left: Friendly graphics included this cut-out figure of a man with a watering can. It refers to the small tenant gardening plots that would remain part of the site.

Bright colors and simple type contributed to the open, friendly look.

BENAROYA HALL CONSTRUCTION ENCLOSURE

Combining the words "edifice" and "edify" into one structure, this construction enclosure for Seattle's new Symphony Hall even included graphics on top, so that people in surrounding high-rise buildings could read them. Pictures and text, mounted on standard scaffolding, showed that the spirit of a building exists before its walls are built.

Design: WPa Inc.; Principal in Charge: Kathy Wesselman; Design: Kathy Wesselman, Anthony Pellecchia, Joel Bakken

Fabrication: SignTech Seattle

Simple rented scaffolding held images, text, and credits. Mounted at angles, the panels were visible from all directions — even from above.

Bright and friendly, the panels presented encouraging words, and images that showed people enjoying and playing music.

THE PIER SOUND AND LIGHT INSTALLATION

This sound and light installation by Hans Peter Kuhn transformed an abandoned concrete bridge into a work of art. Nine illuminated pillars are topped with loudspeakers, which play a computer-controlled collection of sounds recorded from nature.

Artist: Hans Peter Kuhn

Client: Goethe-Institut/German Cultural Center; Director: Dr. Stephan Nobbe

Assistant to Artist: Arno Kraehahn

Production: Christopher Buckley

Assistant: Phil Widmer

Photography: Gerhard Kassner

Manhattan's Pier 32, a condemned concrete bridge, is the setting for this sound and light installation meant to create an air of tranquility.

The illuminated pillars are 15 ft. high, with 6-ft. bases. Because loudspeakers are 300 feet away from listeners, sounds have a muted, distant character.

YOU ARE HERE: GRAPHICS THAT DIRECT, EXPLAIN & ENTERTAIN

DENVER CHILDREN'S MUSEUM 20TH ANNIVERSARY

D esigners created a zoo of wire animal sculptures to hang from a white "circus tent" for a museum's benefit.

Design: Communication Arts, Inc.; Principal in Charge: Henry Beer; Designers: David Tweed, Max Steele, Margaret Sewell

Fabrication: David Tweed

Balloons, colored lights, cut-out numbers, and wire "mobiles" set the scene for a gala benefit dinner.

Three-dimensional wire sculptures brought whimsical animals to life.

Giant signs featuring pictograms served the six-month exposition hosted by Seville, Spain. More than 100 countries were represented, and 40 million people visited from around the world. The system included 30 sign types, 3,000 signs, and 20 custom symbols.

Design: Landor Associates; Design Directors: Michael Collins, Caroline Schroder; Creative Directors: Richard Ford, Patrick Brossollet; Designers: Neil Paterson, Andy Glidden

Fabrication: Mapasa

To communicate with an international audience, designers created 20 detailed icons based on the Expo's architecture and features. These symbols served as the signs' primary "language."

The modular signs, which were used to create 30 sign types, helped visitors navigate a temporary city marked by lush landscaping, a monorail, and fantastic architecture.

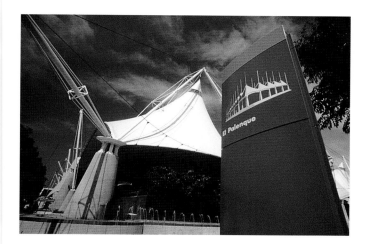

Messages in Spanish and English were hardly adequate to address visitors speaking hundreds of languages.

L ight transformed the facade of Manhattan's landmark Post Office for a Brooklyn Academy of Music gala dinner. Hand-painted glass slides made use of "anamorphosis," a perspective trick that allows viewers to experience different images from different locations on the street.

Design: Leni Schwendinger Light Projects, Ltd.; Artist: Leni Schwendinger; Designers: Leni Schwendinger, David Lander

Client: Brooklyn Academy of Music

Lighting Supplier: Production Arts Lighting

Photography: Robert Hirschberg

Five computer-controlled opera projectors cast multi-layered images onto the facade of a landmark building.

Artwork explored the postal
service and the art of
correspondence, making what
goes on inside the building visible
on its outside face.

SECTION 6
EDUCATIONAL AND CULTURAL ENVIRONMENTS

The Art of Architecture at the Denver Art Museum

Graphics for these projects work on two levels: wayfinding and interpreting. They both "explain and entertain," while addressing an audience of all ages, nationalities and educational backgrounds. Interpretive signs frequently require designers to become instant experts on obscure or difficult subjects. They also require innovative teaching techniques, such as group problem solving. Often these projects meld graphic, exhibit, set, and theater design into a seamless whole.

United States Holocaust Memorial Museum

Fernbank Museum of Natural History, Atlanta

Rock and Roll Hall of Fame Interactive Computer Programs

VIRGINIA AIR & SPACE CENTER

A spacewalking astronaut became the identity symbol for a new museum. The designers created both the signs and print graphics, so that all graphic communications carry the same message.

Design: Whitehouse & Co.; Designers: Mary Elliott, Roger Whitehouse

Architecture: Mitchell Giurgola

Fabrication: ASI Sign Systems

The distinctive building is its own sign. A cutout of an astronaut hanging from the roof and simple letters over the portal both communicate the identity and harmonize with the architecture.

Simple directional signs help users without drawing undue attention to themselves.

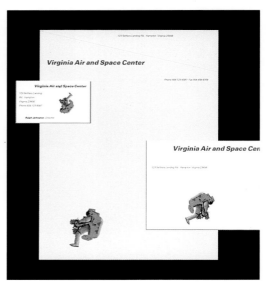

Tumbling through space, where there is no up or down, the astronaut marks all print graphics.

THE POWER OF MAPS *at the Cooper Hewitt Museum*

S igns and display tables shaped like folded maps set the theme for this exhibit. Pentagram designed the signs, structures and exhibition program (which, like a map, unfolded to to display a diagram of the exhibit). These dynamic graphics worked with the maps on display, themselves colorful and graphic, to create a whole that invited visitors to look at familiar objects in an unfamiliar way.

Design: Pentagram, New York; Partner/Graphics: Peter Harrison; Partner/Architect: James Biber

Curator: Lucy Fellowes, Cooper-Hewitt Museum

Fabrication: Rathe Productions

Photography: Peter Mauss, Esto Photographics

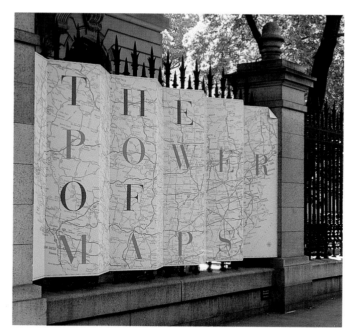

The exterior sign, hung on the museum's fence, provides a preview of both the signs and the exhibits. The whimsical road map of the United States also suggests that the exhibit is a fascinating destination.

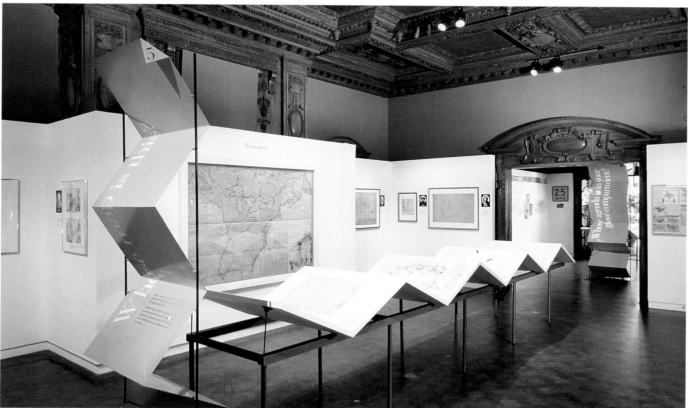

Custom display tables echo the familiar form of a folded map. The maps on display provide a bold and graphic background that allowed designers to make use of bright colors and imposing sizes.

C ut into a Jerusalem hillside and as imposing as the ruins of some long-vanished civilization, this monument commemorates 5,000 Jewish communities destroyed in the Holocaust. Excavated 7 to10 meters into the earth and coated with stone, the maze-like structure represents a map of Europe. Each of the community names is carved or sandblasted into 107 stone walls.

Artifice makes these new walls look as silent and abandoned as ancient ruins. Sandblasted into a hillside, built into structures, then coated with stone, the memorial inspires awe and contemplation.

Custom Hebrew letters, inspired by 2,000-year-old inscriptions, were designed for the project.

The names of 5,000 Jewish communities destroyed in the Holocaust are sandblasted into the wall in both roman and Hebrew letters. The 100,000 letters, each 8 cm. high, were created with computer-generated stencils.

Design: David Grossman and Yaki Molcho; Designers: David Grossman, Yaki Molcho; Associate Graphic Designer: Ofer Landau

Landscape Architects: Dan Zur, Lipa Yahalom

Sandblasting: GRAPH-X

Photography: Ilan Besor

THE CREATIVE DISCOVERY MUSEUM

A n exciting and innovative building in Chattanooga, TN, houses provocative exhibits designed to help children learn creative and critical thinking. Hands-on, interactive experiences are offered in four areas: art, invention, music, and paleontology.

Design: Lee. H. Skolnick Architecture + Design Partnership; Principals: Lee H. Skolnick, Paul Alter; Project Architect: Andrew M. Fethes

Building Team: Miguel Cardenas, Olga Rodriguez, Sergio Paz, Robert Portnoff, Roberta Sloan; Exhibits Team: Jo Ann Secor, Robert Portnoff, Audrey O'Malley, Cynthia Smith, Ellen Leeburger, Cory Munson, Scott Briggs, Jan Schmidt Superstructures: Structural Paradise Technologies; Water Sculpture: Fisher Marantz Renfro Stone; Lighting and HVAC: Altieri; Consulting Engineers: Sebor Wieber

Graphics: Pentagram Design

Photography: Peter Aaron/Esto

The distinctive tower houses optics activities. There are several viewing platforms and a rooftop observatory. The long glass wall allows drivers to peer inside, and lets visitors see the world outside.

An interactive, kinetic sculpture allows museum visitors to be both inside and outside the building.

Interactive displays throughout the museum urge children to explore their senses.

FROM MARS TO MAIN STREET: AMERICA DESIGNS 1965-1990

This exhibit at the National Building Museum in Washington, DC, explored the US federal government's influence on design in eight disciplines: architecture, landscape architecture, interior design, historic preservation, graphic design, product and industrial design, urban design, and engineering.

Designers made use of the high ceilings by creating suspended and tall, freestanding displays.

Left: Artifacts and interpretive graphics worked together to explain and demonstrate the federal government's influence on design.

Design: Lee H. Skolnick Architecture + Design Partnership; Principal in Charge: Lee H. Skolnick; Design Team: Fred Ellman, Cynthia E. Smith; Museum Services Director: Jo Ann Secor

Graphic Design Consultant: Doublespace

Fabrication: R.H. Guest

Photography: Maxwell MacKenzie

Tall red "towers" provided continuity throughout the exhibits.

THOMAS H. KEAN NEW JERSEY STATE AQUARIUM

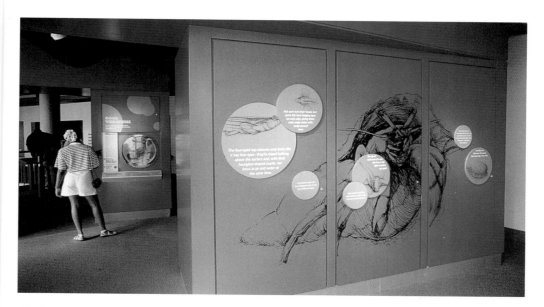

Absolute accuracy is necessary for animal drawings in zoos and aquariums. These interpretive graphics make use of color and shape, as well as text and illustrations, to make their point.

Aquarium visitors can see and even touch some of the animals on display. Interpretive graphics function as part of a whole that includes murals, sounds, and human interaction.

Interactive displays like this one are designed to be used by several people at once. They are informative to people of all ages and educational levels.

This Camden, NJ, facility combines traditional exhibits, including a 750,000-gallon tank aquarium and various smaller habitat-based presentations, with interactive display. The building's second floor is devoted to innovative hands-on, interactive devices and activities.

Design: Joseph A. Wetzel Associates; Principal in Charge/Design: Joseph Wetzel; Principal in Charge/Construction: Howard Litwak; Project Team: Stephen Brown, Debra Sherman, Jan Underhill Ferrara, John Carney, Sherry Proctor Gail Ringel, Molly O'Brien

Architecture: The Hillier Group

Fabrication: Rathe Productions, Inc., The Larson Company, Berry & Homer, Inc.

Video Production: Two Dollars and a Dream

Multi-Media Consultant: C. Brown Systems Design

Photography: Peter Olson

MEDIEVAL SCULPTURE ROOM

Although France has no laws mandating that museums be accessible to the blind, the Musee des Beaux Arts in Arras, France, wanted to make its sculpture room accessible to all patrons. The designers created an attractive system of sandblasted glass panels that include raised letters, Braille, and tactile drawings. Raised text is highlighted in white or gold, while the Braille text is "invisible" — to all but the blind.

Design: Coco Raynes Associates, Inc.; Designers: Coco Raynes, Seth Londergan

Client: Ministere de la Culture-Direction des Musees de France, Federation du Nord de la France des Societes d'Amis des Musees

Fabrication: Sachs Lawlor

Photography: Coco Raynes; Anxo S.A.

The severe museum setting did not call for bright, contemporary graphics, but demanded a restrained, classic design.

c) Patrons are encouraged to touch the sculpture, much of which is displayed at waist-level. The tactile panels are set at 45-degree angles, so they can be read more easily.

b) Unobtrusive to most visitors, the sandblasted glass panels are vitally important to blind patrons. Designers chose black glass to complement the room.

GEOFFREY BEENE UNBOUND

This exhibit for the Fashion Institute of Technology Museum in New York examined 30 years of the designer's work. Innovative displays included a video of a dancer projected, at various times, on three draped scrims.

Design: Design Writing Research; Chief Designer: J. Abbot Miller; Design Associates: David Williams, Hall Smyth

Client: Geoffrey Beene Inc.

Structural Consultant: Alex Manuele

Video Consultant: Judith Barry

Fabrication: Fashion Institute of Technology Crew

Styling Consultant: Geoffrey Beene, Inc.

Photography: Jack Deutsch

Thirty years of Geoffrey Beene designs were displayed on four enormous stairways. The video image of a dancer moved among three draped scrims.

A window advertised the exhibit with a simple, but briefly puzzling, type treatment.

Oversized black disks set off exuberant formal gowns.

JOAN & IRVING HARRIS CONCERT HALL

This Aspen, CO, concert hall is next to the Herbert Bayer Tent, site of the famed International Design Conference at Aspen. Signs are integrated with the contemporary building, and reflect its references to origami.

Design: WPa, Inc.; Designer/Principal in Charge: Kathy Wesselman

Client: City of Aspen, Colorado

Architecture: Harry Teague Architects

Fabrication: Communication Industries

Photography: Thorney Lieberman

The hall's "origami" roof is a reference to the site (next door) where the International Design Conference at Aspen is held.

Signs in a quiet combination of sandblasted concrete, aluminum, and mineral board repeat the reference to folded paper.

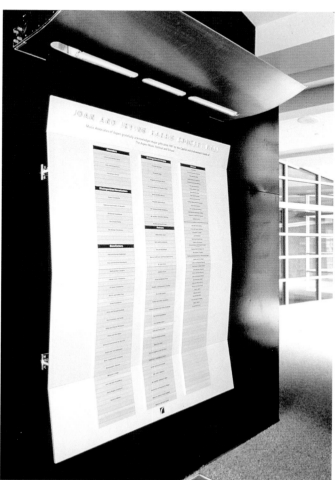

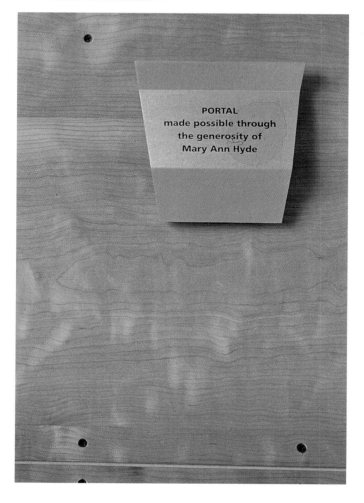

S culpture, architecture and signs combine in this system for a museum in Monterrey, Mexico. In the identity, the final "O" becomes a hollow square. The shape, which suggests the museum's layout, repeats throughout the graphics.

Design: Lance Wyman Ltd.; Principal and Graphic Designer: Lance Wyman; Graphic Designer: Denise Guerra

Banners and other signs repeat the square design.

The museum's logo features a square "O" that suggests its layout — a square building surrounding a central courtyard.

Promotional materials are die-cut with the hollow square.

Below right: The information desk features the identifying hollow square, and also seems to be part of the pillar hanging above it.

This museum is housed in the former keeper's quarters of the Cape Elizabeth, ME, lighthouse. The innovative graphics and displays are part of a restoration and renovation program that met all state historical regulations.

Design: Van Dam Renner Woodworth; Exhibit Designer: Brad Woodworth; Project Manager: Richard Renner; Project Architect: Samuel Van Dam; Modelmaker: F.W. Dixon; Writers: Nancy Brooks, Melissa Kelly, Megan Thorn; Researcher: Christiane Mathan

Client: Town of Cape Elizabeth, Maine

Fabrication: F.W. Dixon, Craig Toffey

Photography: Brian Vanden Brink

The former keeper's quarters beside this historic lighthouse houses an innovative museum.

Information-rich displays include diagrams, artifacts, models, and maps, as well as text and photographs.

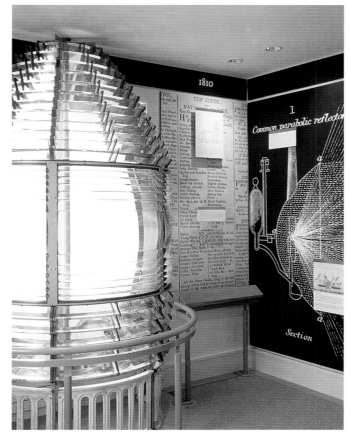

THE ART OF ARCHITECTURE *at The Denver Art Museum*

This two-part exhibit showcased the museum's unique architectural features, and explained its equal focus on architecture and graphics. Gleaming, giant pylons, supergraphics, and dramatic lighting completed the impression of a unique environment.

Design: WPa, Inc.; Graphic Designer: Kathy Wesselman

Architecture: Anthony Pellecchia

Fabrication: Communication Industries, Reed Photo Art, Newcastle Construction

Photography: Thomas Arledge

Architecture or graphic design? The exhibit created a complete environment.

Displays explained the museum's architecture, contents, and history. Photographs, both color and black and white, played a key role in the interpretive graphics.

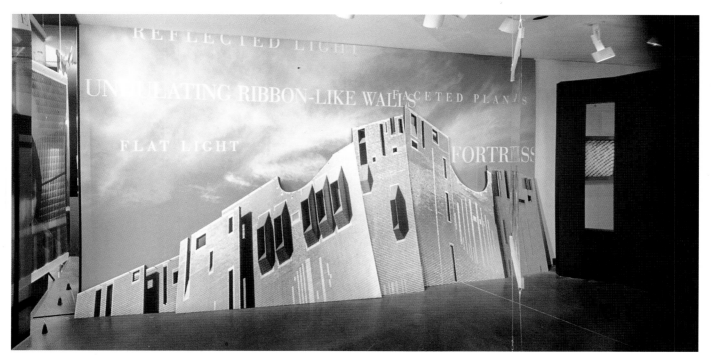

T his comprehensive wayfinding system for the New York museum integrates floor numbers and icons. Print graphics and signs work together to ensure that patrons don't get lost in the giant building.

Design: Lance Wyman Ltd.; Principal: Lance Wyman; Graphic Designer: Denise Guerra; Project Coordinator: Linda Iskander; Draftsman: Ralph Hertle

Fabrication: Mark Fuller Sign Systems

The museum's logo depicts one of its distinctive towers.

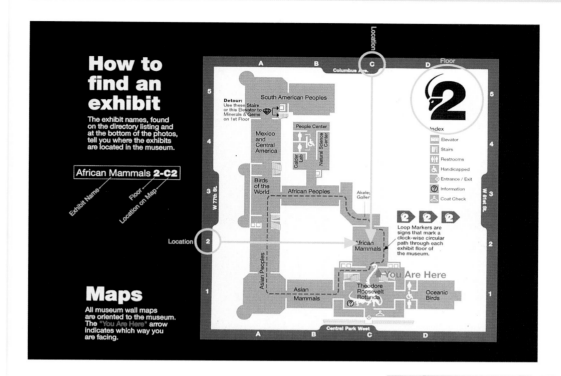

How to find an exhibit

The exhibit names, found on the directory listing and at the bottom of the photos, tell you where the exhibits are located in the museum.

African Mammals **2-C2**

Exhibit Name
Floor
Location on Map

Maps

All museum wall maps are oriented to the museum. The "You Are Here" arrow indicates which way you are facing.

Floor-level arrows help keep visitors on track.

Below: Signs repeat the tower shape. Floor numbers double as icons picturing key exhibits. Each square of the modular sign system can be changed at any time.

S igns are integrated with the classically inspired architecture of this Atlanta museum. An illuminated frieze in the lobby delivers a modern take on nineteenth-century museum design.

Design: Jon Roll & Associates; Principal: Jon Roll; Associate: Denise Lugar; Associate: M.J. Wuest; Designer: Rafael Weil

Architecture: Graham Gund Architects

Fabrication: Designers Workshop

Photography: Jonathan Hillyer

The museum's identity sign matches the restrained, classical lines of its post-modern architecture, and introduces the interior graphics.

Left: An illuminated mural in the lobby recalls nineteenth-century-style design. Strips of recessed letters line the high ceilings, another reference to classic museum design.

Below: Even the most basic of signs are integrated into the architecture.

WORLD OF BIRDS

Innovative when it was designed almost 20 years ago, the Bronx Zoo's 26-environment Lila Acheson Wallace World of Birds needed an update. Extensive renovations combine with new interior architecture and interpretive graphics to bring the building up to date.

Design: Chermayeff & Geismar, Inc.; Principal in Charge: John Grady; Principal Input: Tom Geismar; Designers: Jonathan Alger, Chris Farley, Barbara Kuhr, Chuck Rudy

Client: New York Zoological Society

Architecture: The Stein Partnership

Fabrication: EGAD, F.G.I., Charles M. Maltbie Associates Inc., North Barre Granite, Volmela System Graphics

Photography: Richie Fahey

Drawings of and information about extinct birds is etched into the stone walls.

Extensive interpretive graphics help visitors learn about birds in 26 separate "environments."

A dark, sinuous corridor introduces visitors to the building, and to the study of birds.

C elebrating the 75th anniversary of the 19th amendment to the Constitution of the United States, this massive installation covered the floor of the station's main waiting room. The 8-ft. vinyl letters created a large impact on a small budget.

Design: Drenttel Doyle Partners; Creative Directors: Miguel Oks, Stephen Doyle, William Drenttel; Architectural Designer: James Hicks; Project Manager: Cameron Manning

Client: New York State Division for Women

Fabrication: Volmela System Graphics

Electronic Imagery: Duggal Color Projects

Floor Text: 3M (supplied by Vomela System Graphics)

Photography: Scott Frances

The Amendment's 28 words were reproduced in vinyl letters, some eight ft. long, applied to the marble floor.

Interpretive graphics displayed on a 20-ft. tower exhibit explained some of the history of women's suffrage in the United States.

CHARLES A. DANA DISCOVERY CENTER

Part of New York's Central Park Conservancy, this science education center for children helps visitors launch explorations into the park, and bring things they collect back to a naturalist's "lab" to examine. Steamer trunks house teaching aids, equipment, and activities, and convert to mini laboratories.

Design: Edwin Schlossberg Inc.; Principal in Charge: Edwin Schlossberg; Design Team: Joe Mayer, Erich Rose; Researcher/Writer: Clay Gish

Client: Central Park Conservancy

Fabrication: R.H. Guest, Inc.

Consultant: The Central Park Conservancy Education Department

Photography: Donald Dietz, Matt Wargo

Part of a major restoration of the north end of Central Park, the Discovery Center helps children explore the park and learn about science.

Steamer trunks hold equipment such as microscopes and compasses, and convert to mini laboratories.

Opening to instant acclaim, this Washington, D.C., museum was designed to be viewed as if visitors walked by tables of evidence in a courtroom. It emphasizes individuals, as well as the Holocaust as a whole. The effect is an overwhelming body of evidence, each piece small and discrete.

Design: Ralph Appelbaum Associates; Principal in Charge and Concept/Exhibition Designer: Ralph Appelbaum; Project Manager/Senior Designer: Christopher Miceli; Design Team: James Cathcart, Victor Colom, Kai Chiu, Robert Homack, Shari Berman

Client: United States Holocaust Memorial Museum (USHMM)

Cartographer: Paul Pugliese

Fabrication: Charles M. Maltbie Associates Inc.

Installation Photography: Christopher Miceli, Timothy Hursley, Jeff Goldburg, Esto

An overwhelming display of photographs communicates that millions of individual people were killed in the Holocaust, not just the difficult-to-grasp idea of races or groups.

Rooms and corridors are filled with small, discrete pieces of information — the "evidence" designers envisioned. Artifacts, photos, and text are integrated into an almost seamless whole.

To make the massive amounts of materials seem immediate and approachable, designers used innovative materials and displays. Unframed glass, open metal frames, and spotlighting make the artifacts seem less like museum displays and more like "things" just discovered and unexplored.

MINNESOTA CHILDREN'S MUSEUM

T he St. Paul museum's dedication to "hands-on" activities inspired the new identity and graphics for its new building. Children's hands, bright colors, and custom type create a memorable identity.

Design: Pentagram Design; Design Director and Partner in Charge: Michael Bierut; Project Manager: Tracey Cameron

Client: Ann Bitter and Jeanne Bergeron, Minnesota Children's Museum

Architecture: James/Snow Architects, The Alliance

Hand Photographers: Michael O'Neill, Judy Olausen

Fabrication: Cornelius Architectural Products, Volmela System Graphics

Installation Photography: Don F. Wong

While the metal letters hanging over the building's entry are models of restraint, the 45-ft.-tall illuminated mural stretching along its street frontage is anything but.

Unmistakable large-format graphics cover the auditorium door.

Signs throughout the building feature children's hands, pointing or making symbols, against brightly colored backgrounds.

ROCK AND ROLL HALL OF FAME INTERACTIVE COMPUTER PROGRAMS

F our interactive computer programs expand on the information given in exhibits, letting visitors explore their own interests. Their design echoes the exhibit design.

Design: The Burdick Group; Principals: Bruce Burdick, Susan K. Burdick; Project Director: Bruce Lightbody; Design Team: Stuart McKee, Jerome Goh, Aaron Caplan, Jerome Goh

Client: Rock and Roll Hall of Fame and Museum

Fabrication: Christian Anthony Design & Production

Consultant: Ciber Network Systems

Photography: The Burdick Group

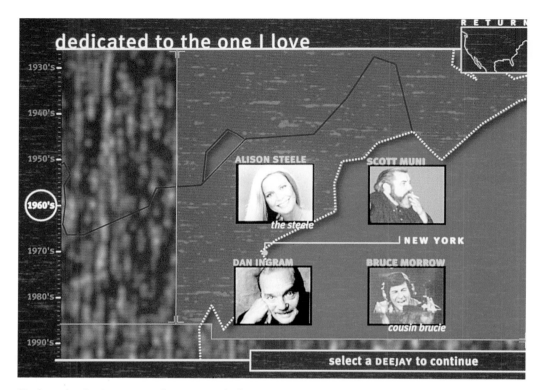

"Dedicated to the One I Love" allows users to find personalities by crosschecking U.S. regions with decades.

The opening graphics for "Come See About Me," a program that allows users to search for artists by name.

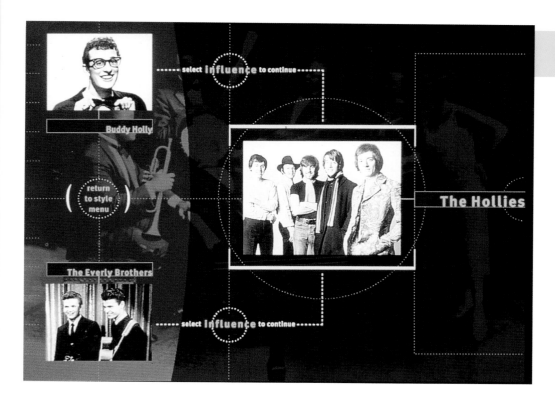

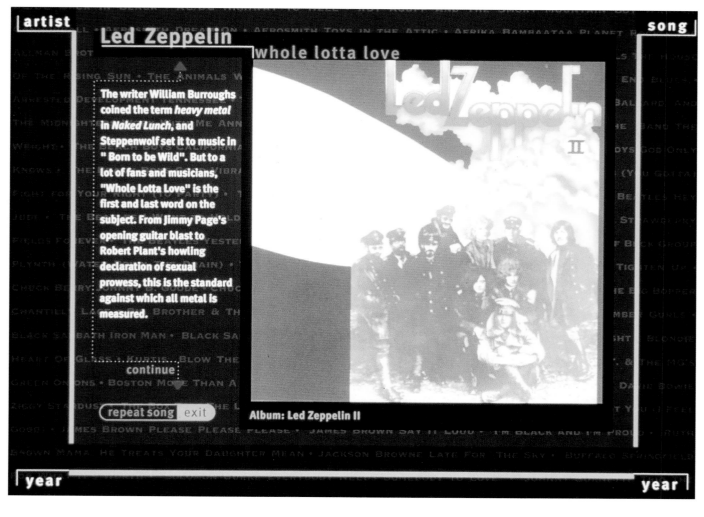

"The Beat Goes On" explores how rock and roll musicians and styles have influenced each other.

Below: "500 Songs that Shaped Rock and Roll" lets users check for songs by group, title and year.

There's one law that said, if somebody is threatening to shoot you, you can report him. But they will not do anything until he actually shot at you. And I think that will actually be too late.

T his public, percent-for-art program in the lobby of a California state government building uses children's words to explore the idea of government. The words and architecture work together to give a voice to children, a group of people often overlooked.

Design: BJ Krivanek Art+Design;
Design Director: BJ Krivanek;
Designer: Joel Breaux

Client: The Riverside Arts Foundation

Fabrication: Fabrication Arts

Consultant: Sonia Baez-Hernandez, urban sociologist

Photography: Jeff Kurt Petersen

Suspended from the beam, metal letters form words describing government as an industrial process. The words and quotations contrast idealistic and realistic ideas about government.

A steel I-beam runs down the center of the installation, suggesting solidity and industry. Supporting the beam are translucent acrylic panels bearing quotations about government from local children.

SCIENCE CITY

An on-the-street exhibit that reveals how cities work, the Science City exhibit for the New York Hall of Science and the National Science Foundation, is a truly interactive piece. Visitors see the depth of water mains with periscopes, look at antennae through telescopes, and read about infrastructure on interpretive signs. The idea is slated to be adopted by science museums throughout the United States.

Design: Chermayeff & Geismar Inc.; Project Designer/Manager: Keith Helmetag; Partner Input: John Grady; Exhibit Concept Input: Jonathan Alger

Fabrication: Dimensional Communications

Photography: Karen Yamauchi

Science City exhibits are bolted to public sidewalks, attached to public light poles, and otherwise integrated into the city street. Signs and other graphics reveal the transformers, water mains, and other hidden infrastructure.

Visitors are invited to look at radio antennae through the telescope as they listen to live transmissions through a radio receiver.

SIGNS OF FUN EXHIBIT

This inexpensive exhibit at Philadelphia's Fabric Workshop and Museum explored the works of architect Steve Izenour. Designed by Izenour, it included old-fashioned illusionist paintings and state-of-the-art World Wide Web graphics.

Design: Venturi, Scott Brown and Associates; Exhibit Design: Steve Izenour; Design: John Izenour, Michael Wommack, Huyen Tran

Photography: Matt Wargo

Simple color printouts (generated in Photoshop) hung on faux-painted false walls.

Below: Visitors could view Yale University's "Still Learning from Las Vegas" web site.

A new museum focusing on news, journalism, and the role of the press in a free society needed a design that would keep pace with technology and the ever-changing nature of news. It presents all of human history as, at one time, "news." Visitors can watch news broadcasts be prepared and recorded, are invited to write and edit news stories in interactive games, and can air their news-related concerns at an ethics center.

Design: Ralph Appelbaum Associates Inc.; Principal in Charge: Ralph Appelbaum; Design Director/Senior Designer: Christopher Miceli; Designers: Kai Tom Chiu, Ricardo Mulero, Yolande Daniels; Graphic Designer: Cheung Tai; Content Coordinator: David Mandel; Editor: Sylvia Juran; Project Administrator: Deborah Wolff; Exterior Architecture: Phillip Tefft, James Cathcart; Exterior Designer: Glenn Kushner

Lighting Consultants: H.M. Brandston & Partners, Inc.; Berner & Brill Lighting Design Inc.; Barbizon

Studio Set Design Implementation: Production Design Group

Audio-Visual Systems: Electrosonic

Films: Joseph Cortina; Charles Guggenheim; Newseum

Artifact Installation: Bessant Studio

Acoustics: Charles M. Salter Associates Inc.; Miller Henning Associates

Engineering: K.C.E. Structural Engineers, P.C.; Bansal & Associates

Fabrication: Charles M. Maltbie Associates, Inc., Sunrise Systems

Photography: Scott Frances/Esto

At the museum's entrance, a giant globe presents the names of prominent newspapers in their own typefaces. News-related quotations line the wall by the stairs.

Computer stations for interactive games sit beneath illuminated front pages, electronic message boards, and a live-feed video newswall.

R estored, reinterpreted, and remounted in 1996, the fourth-floor fossil halls at the American Museum of Natural History are home to many world-renowned specimens. New graphics help communicate new scientific thinking about evolution, and help visitors understand the practice of science.

Design: Ralph Appelbaum Associates Inc.; Principal in Charge: Ralph Appelbaum; Project Director/Senior Designer: Melanie Ide; Content Coordinator: Miranda K. Smith; Art Director/Senior Graphic Designer: Laura Genninger; Designers: Elisabeth Cannell, Douglas Balder; Project Administrator: Francis O'Shea; Graphic Designers: Shari

Berman, David Ortega; Graphics Administrator: Vicci Ward; Editor: Sylvia Juran

Architecture: Kevin Roche John Dinkeloo and Associates

Fabrication: Rathe Productions, Charles M. Maltbie Associates. Inc.

Lighting Design: H.M. Brandston & Partners, Inc.

Video Software: The Chedd-Angier Production Co.

Computer Software: C-Wave

Animation: Hall Train

Audio-Visual Systems: Electrosonic

Castings: Sculpture House Casting

Photography: Scott Frances/Esto Photographics

Above: The Hall of Vertebrate Origins explains how early vertebrates came out of the oceans onto land. Specimens and models are hung overhead, with labels on railings beneath them. All exhibits in the main path can be taken apart with a hex wrench, for special events and dining.

Opposite above: Large amounts of scientific information are presented in discrete graphic "packages," as this Glyptotherium exhibit shows.

Opposite below: An exhibit in the Hall of Mammals and their Extinct Relatives illustrates the kind of science done at the museum — cladistics, the classification of organisms based on their evolution. Skeletons and wire outlines show the evolution of the cave bear.

THE J. PAUL GETTY MUSEUM

Three-dimensional models of the museum complex help people find their way to the right buildings

A comprehensive wayfinding program helps people navigate the numerous buildings at the museum complex. Signs range in size from giant site models to small gallery identification signs. Design and type are consistent throughout.

Design: Getty Museum Exhibition Design Department; Principal in Charge: Merritt Price; Senior Designer: Tim McNeil; Designers: Robert Brown, Nicole Hagedorn

Map Illustrator: Dusty Deyo

Fabrication: Carlson and Co.

Exterior signs identify the buildings, or "pavilions."

The same design sensibility is carried down to the small gallery identifiers.

RODIN TEMPORARY EXHIBITS

A quote from Rodin about his fascination with Michelangelo ran along the corridor wall leading to two concurrent Rodin exhibits, one about Michelangelo's influence on the sculptor. Visitors could pass freely between the exhibits, which were anchored by three graphic scrims that provided an ornate architectural note to the plain gray walls and box-shaped pedestals.

Design: Susan Maxman Architects; Principal in Charge: Missy M. Maxwell, AIA; with Curator Christopher Riopelle

Consultant: Willie Fetchko Graphic Design

Fabrication: The Philadelphia Museum of Art; Vision International; Gibbs Connors Exhibit Graphics and Signage

Lighting Design: George Sexton

Scrims: Vision Graphics

Digital Imaging: Daiji Asani

A giant quotation along one long corridor wall introduced patrons to two temporary exhibits of the works of Auguste Rodin.

From a central introductory room, visitors could enter either exhibit. The larger exhibit featured Michelangelo's influence on the French sculptor, and included plaster casts of some of the Renaissance master's works.

Pedestals at various heights put the sculptures within easy reach. The handrail, at right, includes Braille and audio messages.

Integrated signs for both blind and sighted audiences open the Calais museum's 19th Century Sculpture Room to all. A Braille and audio handrail describes the floor plan and collection to blind audiences, who are permitted to "see" the sculptures with their hands. Photo sensors on the rail trigger audio descriptions that describe the sculptures and their characteristics for all visitors.

Design: Coco Raynes Associates Inc.; Principal in Charge: Coco Raynes; Designers: Coco Raynes, Seth Londergan, Ernest Lorentsov

Consultants: National Systems Inc.

Fabricators: Milgo; Sachs Lawlor

Auguste Rodin
Paris 1840 - Meudon 1917

Tête d'Eustache de Saint-Pierre
Etude pour le Monument
des Bourgeois de Calais - Vers 1886-1887

Bronze. Fonte E. Godard, 1981
Don des Amis du Musée de Calais, 1981
81.13.1

Information about each piece is presented on sandblasted glass panels. For the sighted, letters are paint-filled. Braille letters are left transparent.

The new graphic system makes the sculpture room accessible to the blind, who are permitted to touch the statues as well as read about them.

SECTION 7
CONCEPTUAL PLANS AND STUDENT WORK

Grate Fish Storm Drain, San Francisco

Research, proposals, student work, and identity guidelines have one thing in common: Fabrication, if even possible, is not the most important part of the work. Thinking, planning, studying, and finally creating a new solution to a design problem is the ultimate goal.

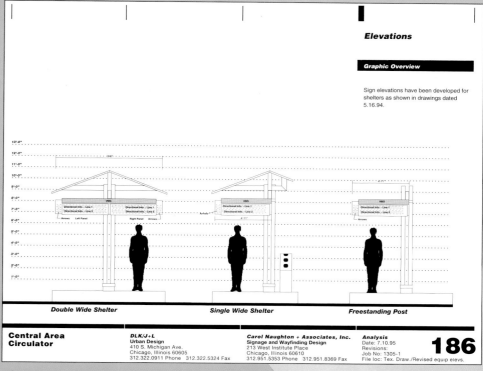

Graphic Overview

Sign elevations have been developed for shelters as shown in drawings dated 5.16.94.

13'-0"
12'-0"
11'-0"
10'-0"
9'-0"
8'-0"
7'-0"
6'-0"
5'-0"
4'-0"
3'-0"
2'-0"
1'-0"

Double Wide Shelter   **Single Wide Shelter**   **Freestanding Post**

| Central Area Circulator | DLK/J+L
Urban Design
410 S. Michigan Ave.
Chicago, Illinois 60605
312.322.0911 Phone   312.322.5324 Fax | Carol Naughton + Associates, Inc.
Signage and Wayfinding Design
213 West Institute Place
Chicago, Illinois 60610
312.951.5353 Phone   312.951.8369 Fax | Analysis
Date: 7.10.95
Revisions:
Job No: 1305-1
File loc: Tex. Draw./Revised equip elevs. | **186** |

Chicago Central Area Circulator Signage and Wayfinding Analysis

Photovoltaic Sunflower Sign

THE RAYNES RAIL

A handrail that provides continuous Braille information was the first major sign innovation to follow the Americans with Disability Act. Tested at The Massachusetts Eye & Ear Infirmary, Boston, the system includes audio devices as well as Braille.

Design: Coco Raynes Associates, Inc.: Inventor/Principal in Charge: Coco Raynes; Design Team: Matt Kanaracus, Karen Leduc

Client: The Massachusetts Eye & Ear Infirmary

Fabrication: New England Plastics

Consultants: Carroll Center for the Blind, Brien Charlson and Betty Gayzaiian; Massachusetts Commission for the Blind, Allan White

Photography: Bill Miles

Braille messages describe traffic patterns, explain directions, and otherwise guide blind users along corridors and through intersections. Audio messages help those who cannot read Braille.

Strips of plastic carry Braille messages along the inner side of the handrails, keeping them safe from vandalism and making them "invisible" to all but their intended audience.

PHOTOVOLTAIC SUNFLOWER SIGN

Designed by a student, this prototype sign for events and festivals uses solar energy, rather than relying on generators or extension cords.

Design: The GNU Group; Designer: Michael Delaney

Advisor to SEGD Student Grant Project: Richard Burns

At night, logos and information glow without using extension cords or generators.

The sign is light, collapsible, and easy to store.

Designed for outdoor events, the freestanding sign looks a little unusual. Solar collectors above the sign store electricity all day.

This study analyzed circulation and wayfinding requirements for Chicago's Field Museum of Natural History.

Design: Carol Naughton + Associates, Inc.; Designers: Carol Naughton, Edward Kuliesis

Client: Holabird & Root

Information/Reception Orientation

The location of the Information/Reception desk should act as a central locator in the building.

Current Configuration
The existing configuration of the information sequence is as follows:
1. The visitor purchases a ticket at the north or south entry.
2. The visitor then organizes how they would plan their visit, by finding the information desk.

The existing configuration has no existing advance organizers to allow the visitor to plan their own itinerary.

New South Main Entrance Configuration
The South main entry configuration of the information sequence would follow:
1. The visitors could be given advance organizers, which could be located in the hallway at the south end or in the hallway at the north end. This would allow the visitor to plan their visit. The limited amount of space in these areas needs to be expanded to tell a complete story about the museum and its exhibits. Exits at this area would provide egress for visitors leaving and avoid 2-way traffic congestion.
2. The visitor purchases a ticket at the information reception desk.

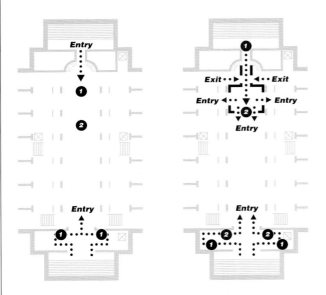

Carol Naughton + Associates, Inc.
213 West Institute Place
Chicago, Illinois 60610
312.951.5353 Phone   312.951.8369 Fax

Job Number: 1710.3
Disk Name: Field Museum
Folder Name: 1710.3 Field Museum
File Name: Master plan

Analysis
Scale: N.T.S.
Date: 6.23.95
Revisions: 7.21.95

19

CHICAGO CENTRAL AREA CIRCULATOR SIGNAGE AND WAYFINDING

T his study analyzed sign and wayfinding requirements for a proposed expansion to Chicago's light rail system.

Design: Carol Naughton + Associates, Inc.; Designers: Carol Naughton, Vick Moore, Julie Kimball

Client: DLK/J+L Urban Design Team, City of Chicago

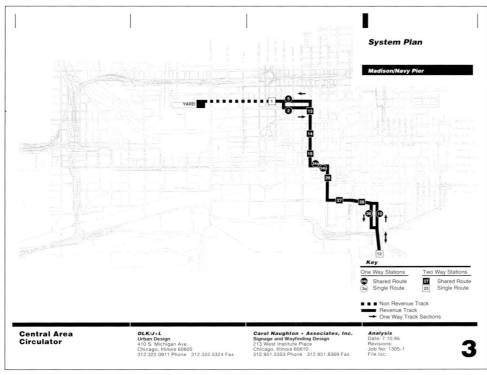

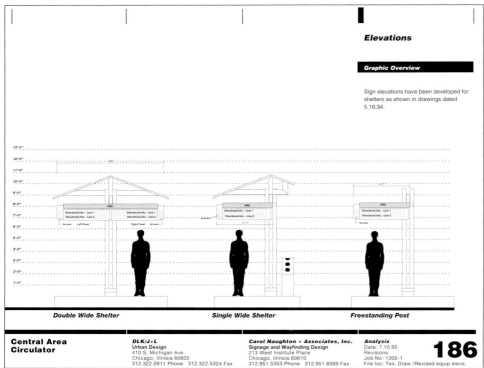

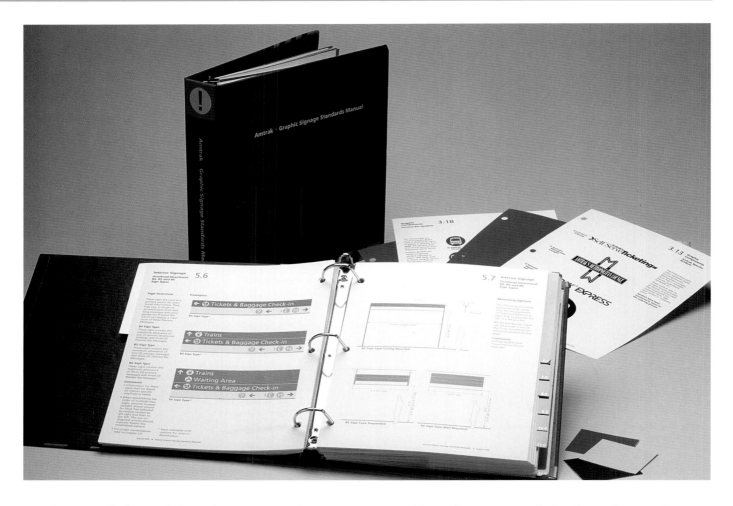

This new standards manual, designed to create a "seamless Amtrak" look in many different stations, was commissioned to help the railway system comply with the Americans with Disabilities Act.

Design: The McCulley Group; Principal: John Riley McCulley; Design Team: Nicholas A. Grohe; Diana Duque

Client: Amtrak, National Railroad Passenger Corporation; I. Suzi Andiman

Consultants/Fabrication: Architectural Graphics, Inc. (AGI); Harry Weese Associates; DeWitt & Associates

E xisting highway signs use seven different typestyles, only one in both upper- and lower-case. That face is difficult for aging drivers to read. The study tested numerous typefaces, and results included a new design, as well as more data on often-asserted but seldom-proved concepts such as whether mixed-case faces are really easier to read.

Design: Meeker & Associates, Inc.; Design Team: Donald T. Meeker, Christopher O'Hara, Harriet Spear

Client: Pennsylvania Transportation Institute (with assistance from 3M); Martin Pietrucha, Ph.D., Research Director; Phillip Garvey, Principal Investigator; Susan T. Chrysler, Ph.D., 3M Senior Human Factors Engineer

Consultant: Terminal Design, Inc.; James Montalbano

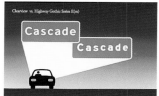

Computer graphics simulated typefaces at various distances and under various light conditions.

Left: Drivers compared typefaces on a test track, for "real world" results.

Below: A new typeface, Clearview, solves many of the problems aging drivers encounter when reading traditional highway typefaces.

SHELTER

S tarting a new summer Farmer's Market, the Charlotte, NC, Uptown Development Corporation expected 100 vendors each weekend. To avoid problems with setup and breakdown, and to help vendors avoid rental charges, the agency hired designers to create an affordable foldable tent design.

Design: Wagner Murray Architects; Designer: David K. Wagner

Client: Uptown Development Corp.

Fabrication: Erdle Perforating, Inc.

Awnings: Austin Canvas Specialties

Photography: Catherine Bauknight, Stanley Capps

Shelter tents can be put up and taken down in less than three minutes. Awning fabric attaches to the aluminum frame with Velcro. At less than $300, each tent costs significantly less than rental fees for standard four-post tents.

Right: Shelter tents can be used individually, or combined in various configurations.

When massed together, the tents create a colorful environment.

YOU ARE HERE: GRAPHICS THAT DIRECT, EXPLAIN & ENTERTAIN

LONDON UNDERGROUND SIGN MANUAL

P art of a complete corporate identity system, this sign manual for the 285-station London Underground subway capped an eight-year redesign.

Design: Henrion, Ludlow & Schmidt; Project Director: Chris Ludlow; Designers: David Clacy, Sally Munro

Fabrication: Burnham & Co. (Onyx) Ltd.

One of the world's most familiar corporate identity marks, the Underground's circle and bar combination remains unchanged — as does the world-famous map system.

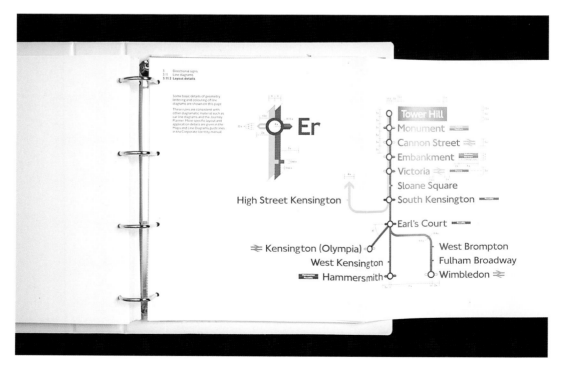

This design for San Francisco's streets was meant to solve the ongoing problem of people dumping automobile oil into the storm drains and polluting San Francisco Bay. Stenciled warnings near existing drains, the designer felt, need constant maintenance and do little to deter people who already know they shouldn't dump.

Design: Mauk Design; Principal in Charge: Mitchell Mauk

The proposed grate, shaped like a fish, would graphically challenge people by making their dirty deed concrete: making them dump oil on a fish.

MIRAGES OF WALLS

This project by a student at Pratt Institute converted computer pixels into black, white, and gray tiles. The concept is illustrated with a design for the walls at the 42nd Street Subway Station in New York, featuring the faces and feet taken from a vintage photo of the Ziegfeld Follies dancers who became synonymous with the area.

Design: Piotr Adamski

In this design for subway station walls, faces of Ziegfeld Follies dancers are rendered in black, white and gray tile.

To convey the scale of his design — the entire length of the 42nd Street Station — the designer used a mathematical trick, a spiral presentation that fools the viewer into seeing the drawings in perspective and in context. This second, flat presentation of the design alone was also available for viewing.

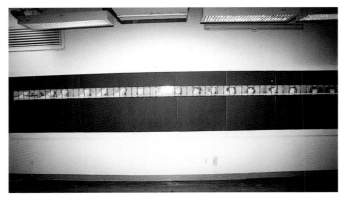

Up close, this dancer's foot reveals its origin in computer pixels.

INDEX OF DESIGN FIRMS

Goethe Institute
(for Hans Peter Kuhn)
German Cultural Center
1014 Fifth Avenue
New York, NY 10028
Phone: 212-439-8700
Fax: 212-439-8705
• Page: 130

Gottschalk & Ash International
11 Bishop Street
Toronto, Ontario M5R 1N3
CANADA
Phone: 416-963-9717
Fax: 416-963-9351
• Pages: 60-61, 110

David Grossman & Yaki Molcho
Rehov Vital 12
Tel Aviv, 66088
ISRAEL
Phone: 972/36812715
Fax: 972/36812716
• Pages: 140-141

Group/Chicago, Inc.
400 W. Erie Street. #302
Chicago, IL 60610
Phone: 312-787-4504
Fax: 312-787-4942
• Page: 84

Henrion, Ludlow & Schmidt
12 Hobart Place
London, SW1W 0HH
UNITED KINGDOM
Phone: 44-171-235-5466
• Page: 191

HKS Inc.
1919 McKinney Avenue
Dallas, TX 75201-1753
Phone: 214-969-5599
Fax: 214-969-3387
• Page: 52

Interbrand Corporation
437 Madison Avenue, 10th Floor
New York, NY 10022
Phone: 212-366-6969
Fax: 212-752-4503
• Page: 82

Jon Roll Associates
48 Dunster Street
Cambridge, MA 02138
Phone: 617-868-5430
• Pages: 42, 158-159

Joseph A. Wetzel Associates, Inc.
77 North Washington Street
Boston, MA 02114
Phone: 617-367-6300
Fax: 617-742-8722
• Page: 145

Keith Muller Associates
56 The Esplanade, Suite 510
Toronto, Ontario M5E 1A7
CANADA
Phone: 416-362-6446
• Pages: 60-61, 110

Hans Peter Kuhn
c/o Goethe Institute
German Cultural Center
1014 Fifth Avenue
New York, NY 10028
Phone: 212-439-8700
Fax: 212-439-8705
• Page: 130

Lance Wyman Ltd.
118 West 80th Street
New York, NY 10024
Phone: 212-580-3010
Fax: 212-874-6814
• Pages: 150-151, 156-157

Landmark Entertainment Group
5200 Lankershim Blvd. #700
North Hollywood, CA 91601
Phone: 818-753-6700
Fax: 818-753-6767
• Pages: 70-71

Landor Associates
1001 Front Street
San Francisco, CA 94111
Phone: 415-955-1201
Fax: 415-391-9563
• Pages: 20-21, 132-133

Lee H. Skolnick Architecture +
Design Partnership
7 West 22nd Street, 10th Floor
New York, NY 10010
Phone: 212-989-2624
Fax: 212-727-1702
• Pages: 142-143, 144

Leni Schwendinger Light Projects, Ltd.
459 West 35th Street
Studio B
New York, NY 10001
Phone: 212-947-6282
Fax: 212-947-6289
• Pages: 134-135

Lorenc Design
724 Longleaf Drive, NE
Atlanta, GA 30342-4307
Phone: 404-266-2711
Fax: 404-233-5619
• Pages: 8-9

Mauk Design
39 Stillman Street
San Francisco, CA 94107
Phone: 415-243-9277
Fax: 415-243-9278
• Pages: 89, 90-91, 100-101, 192

Mayer/Reed
319 SW Washington
Suite #820
Portland, OR 97204
Phone: 503-223-5953
Fax: 503-223-8076
• Pages: 10, 12-13, 44-45

The McCulley Group
434 West Cedar Street
San Diego, CA 92101
Phone: 619-236-8700
Fax: 619-847-8143
• Page: 188

McMillan Group, Inc.
111 Westport Avenue
Norwalk, CT 06851
Phone: 203-846-9648
Fax: 203-847-8143
• Pages: 102-103

Meeker & Associates, Inc.
22 Rockwood Drive
Larchmont, NY 10538
Phone: 914-834-1904
Fax: 914-834-1927
• Page: 189

Yaki Molcho & David Grossman
Rehov Vital 12
Tel Aviv, 66088
ISRAEL
Phone: 972/36812715
Fax: 972/36812716
• Pages: 140-141

Morla Design
463 Bryant Street
San Francisco, CA 94107
Phone: 415-543-6548
Fax: 415-543-7214
• Page: 98

NBBJ
(for Salestrom Design)
111 South Jackson Street
Seattle, WA 98104
Phone: 206-621-2390
Fax: 206-621-2305
• Pages: 112-113

The Office of Michael Manwaring
111 Crescent Road
San Anselmo, CA 94960
Phone: 415-458-8100
Fax: 415-458-8105
• Pages: 66-67, 121

Pentagram Design
204 Fifth Avenue
New York, NY 10010
Phone: 212-683-7000
Fax: 212-532-0181
• Pages: 58, 59, 74-75, 96, 139, 166-167

Perkins & Will Environmental
Graphic Design
330 North Wabash
Chicago, IL 60611
Phone: 312-755-0770
Fax: 312-755-0755
• Pages: 40-41

Poulin/Morris
286 Spring Street, 6th Floor
New York, NY 10013
Phone: 212-675-1332
Fax: 212-675-3027
• Pages: 17, 18-19, 24, 36-37

Pratt Institute
(for Piotor Adamski)
116 E. 7th Street, #6
New York, NY 10009
Phone: 212-529-5323
• Page: 193

PUBLIK Information Design
Box 3487, 349 West Georgia
Vancouver, BC V6B 344
CANADA
Phone: 604-331-0358
Fax: 604-331-0358
• Page: 128

Ralph Appelbaum Associates
133 Spring Street
New York, NY 10012
Phone: 212-334-8200
Fax: 212-334-6214
• Pages: 164-165, 174-175, 176-177

RTKL Associates, Inc.
The Heal's Building
196 Tottenham Court Road
London W1P 9LD
UNITED KINGDOM
• Pages: 72-73

Selbert Perkins Design Collaborative
2067 Massachusetts Avenue
Cambridge, MA 02140
Phone: 617-497-6605
Fax: 617-661-5772
• Page: 97

Skidmore, Owings & Merrill LLP
One Front Street
San Francisco, CA 94111
Phone: 415-981-1555
Fax: 415-398-3214
• Page: 26

Spagnola and Associates
4 West 22nd Street
New York, NY 10010
Phone: 212-807-8113
Fax: 212-366-5632
• Pages: • Pages: 50-51

Susan Maxman Architects
123 South 22nd Street
Philadelphia, PA 19103
Phone: 215-977-8662
Fax: 215-977-9742
• Page: 179

Susan Roberts: Art Color Design
University of Georgia/
Visual Arts Building
Athens, GA 30602
Phone: 706-542-1511
Fax: 706-542-0226
• Pages: 56-57

Sussman/Prejza & Co. Inc.
8520 Warner Drive
Culver City, CA 90232
Phone: 310-836-3939
Fax: 310-836-3980
• Pages: 16, 68-69, 80-81, 111

Tom Graboski Associates
4649 Ponce de Leon Blvd. #401
Coral Gables, FL 33146
Phone: 305-669-2550
Fax: 305-669-2539
• Pages: 30-31

Two Twelve Associates
596 Broadway, Suite 1212
New York, NY 10012
Phone: 212-925-6885
Fax: 212-925-6988
• Page: 53

Van Dam Renner Woodworth
151 Newbury Street
Portland, ME 04101
Phone: 207-774-0185
Fax: 207-774-8394
• Pages: 152-153

Venturi, Scott Brown and Assoc.
4236 Main Street
Philadelphia, PA 19127-1696
Phone: 215-487-0400
Fax: 215-487-2520
• Pages: 46-47, 172-173

Wagner Murray Architects, PA
437 South Tryon Street
Charlotte, NC 28202
Phone: 704-372-8603
Fax: 704-335-0361
• Page: 190

Whitehouse & Company
18 East 16th Street
Suite 700
New York, NY 10003
Phone: 212-206-1080
Fax: 212-727-2150
• Page: 138

Wieber Nelson Design
2323 Broadway, Studio 201
San Diego, CA 92102
Phone: 619-239-2312
Fax: 619-239-2313
• Page: 124

WPa, Inc.
911 Western Avenue
Suite 380
Seattle, WA 98104
Phone: 206-233-0550
Fax: 206-233-0663
• Pages: 129, 148-149, 154-155

RESOURCE DIRECTORY

Adelphia Graphic Systems (AGS)
302 Commerce Drive
Exton, PA 19341
Phone: 610-363-8150
Fax: 610-363-7029
e-mail: agspa@aol.com
Contact Person: Mr. Alan Jacobson
Page: 111

Ampersand Contract Signing Group
3400 San Fernando Road
Los Angeles, CA 90065
Phone: 213-255-1102
Fax: 213-255-2848
Contact Person: Mr. Randolph
Hampton
Pages: 62-63

Andco Industries Corporation
4100 Sheraton Court
Greensboro, NC 27410
Phone: 910-299-4511 or
800-476-8900
Fax: 910-299-4700
e-mail: frankie@andco.com
Internet: http://www.andco.com
Contact: Frankie D. Perry or
Robert H. Allen, Jr.
Pages: 12-13

Architectural Graphics, Inc.
2655 International Parkway
Virginia Beach, VA 23452
Phone: 757-427-1900
Fax: 757-430-1297
e-mail: rsg@agisign.com
Contact Person: Ms. Robin Garrett
Pages: 20-21, 52, 68-69, 111, 188

Ariston
485 Bloy Street
Hillside, NJ 07205
Phone: 800-526-4901
Fax: 908-687-4880
e-mail: LBonsper@aol.com
Contact Person: Mr. Lee Bonsper
Page: 125

California Neon Products
c/o CNP Sign Company
4530 Mission Gorge Place
San Diego, CA 92120
Phone: 619-283-2191
Fax: 619-283-9503
e-mail: BMCCarter@CNPSign.com
Contact Person: Mr. Bob McCarter
Pages: 105, 124

Carlson & Co.
13023 Arroyo Street
San Fernando, CA 91340
Phone: 818-898-9796
Fax: 415-898-9786
e-mail: Carlsonandco.com
Contact Person: Mr. Mark Nelsen
Pages: 16, 68-69, 178

Colite International, Ltd.
229 Parson Street
West Columbia, SC 29169
Phone: 803-926-7926
Fax: 803-926-8412
e-mail: Colite@msn.com
Contact Person: Mr. Martin Brown
Pages: 20-21

Gibbs Connors Exhibit Graphics and
Signage
235 South Quince Street
Philadelphia, PA 19107
Phone: 215-922-5767
Fax: 215-922-7158
Contact Person: Mr. Gibbs Connors
Page: 179

Cornelius Architectural Products, Inc.
30 Pine Street
Pittsburgh, PA 15223
Phone: 412-781-9003
Fax: 412-781-7840
Contact Person: Mr. Michael Kranack
Pages: 62-63, 166-167

Design & Production Incorporated
7110 Rainwater Place
Lorton, VA 22079
Phone: 703-550-8640
Fax: 703-339-0296
e-mail: DPLorton@aol.com
Contact Person: Mr. Michael D.
Smith
Page: 15

Enameltec - Porcelain Signage
60 Armstrong Avenue
Georgetown, Ontario L7G 4R9
CANADA
Phone: 905-873-1677
Fax: 905-873-9617
e-mail: jen@enameltec.com
Contact Person: Ms. Jennifer
Fairclough
Pages: 112-113

Fireform Porcelain, Inc.
368 Yolanda Avenue
Santa Rosa, CA 95404
Phone: 707-523-0580
Fax: 707-546-4022
e-mail: fireform@sonic.net
Contact Person: Mr. Grant Baughman
Pages: 24, 121

Fun Display
65A Elmira Street
San Francisco, CA 94124
Phone: 415-468-3861
Fax: 415-468-3862
Contact Person: Mr. Craige A. Walters
Page: 98

Livart Incorporated
2 Smith Street
Greenlawn, NY 11740
Phone: 800-582-5812
Fax: 516 261 9504
e-mail: livart@aol.com
Internet: http://www.livart.com
Contact: Mr. Albert Mantaring or
Ms. Amy Kasindorf
Page: 53

Charles M. Maltbie Associates, Inc.
708 Fellowship Road
Mt. Laurel, NJ 08054
Phone: 609-234-0052
Fax: 609-234-0760
e-mail: cmaltbie@maltbie.com
Contact Person: Mr. Charles M.
Maltbie, Jr.
Pages: 160, 164-165, 174-175,
176-177

Media Projects International, Ltd
7 Cameron House
12 Castlehaven Road
London NW1 8QW
UNITED KINGDOM
Phone: 44-171-485-5657
Fax: 44-171-482-4995
e-mail: info@mediaprojects.co.uk
Contact Person: Ms. Rosalie Vickers-
Harris
Page: 72-73

Ostrom Glass & Metal Works
2170 N. Lewis
Portland, OR 97227
Phone: 503-281-6469
Fax: 503-284-9245
Contact Person: Ms. Linda Showman
Page: 45

Philadelphia Sign Company
707 West Spring Garden Street
Palmyra, NJ 08065
Phone: 609-829-1460
Fax:: 609-829-8549
Contact Person: Mr. Wright L. Rundle
Pages: 20-21

Rathe Productions, Inc.
555 West 23rd Street
New York, NY 10011
Phone: 212-242-9000
Fax: 212-242-5676
e-mail: rpirnr@worldnet.att.net
Contact Person: Mr. Robert Rathe
Pages: 92-93, 139, 145, 176-177

Sign Management Consultants, Inc.
25 Century Blvd., Suite 606
Nashville, TN 37214
Phone: 615-885-1661
Fax: 615-885-1703
e-mail: pbain@signmgmt.com
Contact Person: Mr. Paul Bain
Pages: 20-21

Signal Sign Company
111 Dorsa Avenue, PO Box 777
Livingston, NJ 07039
Phone: 973-535-9277
Fax: 973-535-9276
e-mail: signalsign@worldnet.att.net
Contact Person: Mr. Bruce J. Fish
Pages: 20-21

Signs & Decal Corp.
410 Morgan Avenue
Brooklyn, NY 11211
Phone: 718-486-6400
Fax: 718-388-3166
e-mail: signsdecal@aol.com
Contact Person: Mr. Babu Khalfan
Pages: 18-19, 34-35, 36-37, 50-51,
112-113

Signtech Seattle
6306 215th Street SW
Mountlake Terrace, WA 98043
Phone: 425-775-7444 or
800-811-7356
Fax: 425-775-2505
e-mail: signtech@signtechseattle.com
Contact: Mr. Russ Roberts or
Mr. Clayton Moss
Pages: 70-71, 129

South Bay Bronze and Aluminum
Foundry, Inc.
PO Box 3254
San Jose, CA 95156
Phone: 408-947-0607
Fax: 408-947-0697
Internet:
http://www.southbaybronze.com
Contact Person: Mr. Gilbert V.
Hernandez
Page: 121

Sunrise Systems, Inc.
575 Washington Street
Pembroke, MA 020359
Phone: 781-826-9706
Fax: 781-826-0061
Contact Person: Mr. Henry C.
Appleton
Pages: 46-47, 50-51, 174-175

Thomas-Swan Sign Co., Inc.
1117 Howard Street
San Francisco, CA 94103
Phone: 415-621-1511
Fax: 415 621 0481
e-mail: swansigns@aol.com
Contact Person: Mr. Ray Paul
Pages: 20-21, 26, 121

Vision International
3030 West Directors Row
Salt Lake City, UT 84104
Phone: 801-973-8929
Fax: 801-973-8944
e-mail: gcchambers@vision-xxl.com
Contact Person: Mr. Gene Chambers
Page: 179

Vomela System Graphics
274 E. Fillmore Ave.
St. Paul. MN 55122
Phone: 800-645-1012
Fax: 612-228-2295
e-mail: joeh@vomela.com
Contact Person: Mr. Joe Hendershot
Pages: 160, 161, 166-167

Wallach Glass Studio
1580 Sebastopol Rd.
Santa Rosa, CA 95407
Phone: 707-527-1205
Fax: 707-573-1493
e-mail: cwal72957@aol.com
Contact Person: Frances Palmer-
Bhendile
Pages: 53, 62-63

RELATED BOOKS FROM ST PUBLICATIONS

ST PUBLICATIONS, INC.
CINCINNATI, OHIO

SIGN GALLERY INTERNATIONAL

From the Editors of Signs of the Times

The whole world uses signs to identify businesses, direct traffic and inform the public. This edition contains nearly 400 full-color photos and descriptive captions in three languages: English, Spanish and Portuguese. The types of signs include:

• Electric signs and channel letters
• Neon signage, graphics and art
• Digital displays
• Carved, routed and gilded signs
• Digitally printed banners
• Large-scale wall murals and more

Sign Gallery International provides the photos and descriptions that will help anyone to better design and fabricate signs.
ISBN 0-944094-33-3

NEON WORLD

By Dusty Sprengnagel
Introduction by Rudi Stern

Neon is the most exciting and effective medium of signage and architectural embellishment available. Since its development at the turn of the century, neon has become an integral part of our urban experience, and the very visual definition of urban centers such as Times Square, Hong Kong and Las Vegas. Neon sign designer Dusty Sprengnagel has travelled the world, photographing the best neon signage and graphics he's seen. The best of those photos, a total of more than 400, are collected in *Neon World*, along with selected signs, graphics and other neon works produced by Sprengnagel's company, Neonline.
ISBN 0-944094-26-0

THE NEW LET THERE BE NEON

by Rudi Stern

Since its development at the turn of the century, neon has become an integral part of our urban experience, and the very visual definition of urban centers. This classic book explores the "light of the American dream" in all its raucous glory. *The New Let There Be Neon* is the only book in which neon is studied both as a handcraft and artistic medium with its own expressive potential. The only comprehensive visual history of neon, this book will delight and inspire anyone interested in the contemporary arts, especially designers, architects, sculptors, and of course, sign designers and fabricators.
ISBN 0-944094-16-3

IN-STORE SIGNAGE & GRAPHICS

By Larry Ruderman with Arthur Ruderman

This exciting new book is about bringing any retail store's vision and identity to life through effective use of in-store signage and graphics. Full-color case studies and graphics-specific in-store photos brilliantly illustrate how you can make any retail environment easier and more fun to shop. From establishing the store as a brand selling merchandise, to marketing opportunities, demographics and more, this book guides the reader through the many choices of effective in-store signage and graphics.
ISBN 0-944094-31-7

VISUAL MERCHANDISING

From the Editors of VM+SD
Visual Merchandising and Store Design

The winners of the *VM+SD* International Visual Merchandising competition are featured in this collection of more than 300 full-color photos of excellent in-store merchandising designs. This book shows excellence in all facets of retail display, including mannequins and forms, signage, lighting, store windows, point-of-purchase merchandising, storewide promotions, apparel accessories, home goods, collateral material, seasonal merchandising and more.
ISBN 0-944094-24-4

STORES AND RETAIL SPACES

From the Editors of VM+SD and
The Institute of Store Planners (ISP)

This collection of 300 full-color photos of excellent and varied designs of more than 60 leading-edge stores features:

• New, renovated stores and specialty shops
• Department stores and kiosks
• Restaurants and entertainment spaces
• Supermarkets and mass merchandise stores.
Selected by top professionals in the visual merchandising and store design fields, *Stores and Retail Spaces* will provide valuable retail design information and inspiration.
ISBN 0-944094-29-5

MORE BOOKS AVAILABLE FROM ST PUBLICATIONS

SIGN DESIGN AND FABRICATION

Commercial Sign Techniques: Step-by-Step

Engineering Sign Structures: An Introduction to Analysis and Design

Gold Leaf Techniques 4th Edition

Mastering Layout

Sign Design and Layout

Sign Design Gallery 2

Sign Gallery

Sign User's Guide: A Marketing Aid

Vinyl Graphics How-to: Master Principles

Vinyl Graphics & Auto Decor Video Instruction Series

RETAIL DESIGN AND VISUAL MERCHANDISING

Budget Guide to Retail Store Planning & Design

Jewelry on Display

Signs That Sell

Visual Merchandising and Store Design Workbook

NEON DESIGN AND FABRICATION

The Light Artist Anthology: Neon and related media

Neon Techniques 4th Edition

Neon: The Next Generation

For a complete catalog of book and trade journal publications, contact:

ST Publications, Inc.
407 Gilbert Avenue
Cincinnati, Ohio 45202
U.S.A.
Tel. 1-800-421-1321 or 513-421-2050
Fax 513-421-5144 or 513-421-6110
E-mail: books@stpubs.com
Website: www.stpubs.com

ST PUBLICATIONS, INC.
CINCINNATI, OHIO